Copyright © – Clodagh Samantha Higgins & Sarah Louise Rutherford 2010

This book is copyright. No part of this book may be reproduced or transmitted in any form by any means, electronic, or mechanical, including photocopying, recording or by any information storage or retrieval system, without prior permission in writing from the publisher. The Australian Copyright Act 1968 (the ACT) allows a maximum of one Chapter or 10% of the book (whichever is greater) to be photocopied by any educational institution for its educational purposes provided that the educational institution (or body that administers it) has given a remuneration notice to Copyright Agency Limited (CAL) under the Act. If you are unsure of your rights, please take your enquiries to the publisher, Clodagh Samantha Higgins & Sarah Louise Rutherford and The Single Man's manual.

Disclaimer: The material in this publication is of the nature of general comment only and does not represent professional advice. It is not intended to provide specific guidance for particular circumstances and it should not be relied on as a basis for any decisions to take action on any matter that it covers. Readers should obtain professional advice where appropriate, before making any such decisions. To the maximum extent permitted by the law, contributors, the author and publishers disclaim all responsibility and liability to any person, arising directly or indirectly from any person taking or not taking action based upon the information in this publication. The names of people in this book have been changed.

Sydney Australia

Editing by LHA Production

sales@thesinglemanslifemanual.com

ISBN 978-0-646-52589-1

We dedicate this book to all the men in our lives that inspired us.

We would like to thank our family and friends for their love and support that helped us make this possible.

Clodagh & Sarah

The Single Man's Manual

Contents

1	Introduction - Starting Over
2	Confidence & Positive Mental Attitude
3	Hobbies / Interests / Art & Culture
4	Social Interaction & Friends
5	Fitness
6	Nutrition
7	Taking Care of Yourself – Inside & Outside
8	Online World – Social & Dating
9	Back on the Dating Scene Again
10	What Next?

Chapter One

Introduction

When a relationship breaks down and people decide to go their separate ways, everyone involved is faced with many new decisions and challenges.

To top the emotions of the separation, there are practical issues such as setting up new residencies, sorting out money, existing property and arranging for care of any children.

Separation creates many changes to your life. It can seem literally, that your whole world has been turned upside-down. The journey to a new life can be difficult even if both parties amicable.

Back in 2007, according to the Australian Bureau of Statistics - 47,963 divorces were granted.

Of those divorces 27.5% were initiated by men, woman in initiated 38.7%, and 33.7% were mutual decisions. So as you can see from these figures, women have been in the majority when it comes to ending a relationship.

Of all the couples, just over half had children.

The average age of men was 44 years.

The average marriage was just on nine years.

So?   Well what this means is - You are not alone.

Many people compare the feeling of separation to grieving the death of a close relative or friend.

There are many men report that separation is even harder to manage.

Separation not only means the loss of a partner, it can also include loss of family unit, home, friends, social life and can extend to the loss of involvement or contact with your children.

Separation is not easy and if the decision was not a joint one, it can be even more difficult. Small tasks like shopping and managing children can add to the stress of the break-up.

Starting a new life is not always as easy as it seems. The mental and emotional impact of the relationship break up can test your strength and ability to start again. However the rewards of going through this journey can change you and your life for the better in the long term.

Moving On From Past Relationships

"Nobody can go back and start a new beginning, but anyone can start today and make a new ending."

Maria Robinson

The mind is a funny thing! It can play tricks on you and even block out the bad memories you had from your previous relationship and only recalling the good times.

Have a think! Was I really happy in the relationship? Spend time thinking about the reasons why you split up.

 Write down some of the things you come up with. This will help to clear your mind.

It is important to talk about the breakdown of your relationship with your family and close friends. They are the people who are there for you most and will keep your mind positive.

It is generally a good idea not to talk to your the same friends that you share with your ex-partner. Involving them can put them in an awkward position and you may find it harder to take a step forward.

Think twice about going to the same places that you used to go to with your ex-partner. You don't necessarily want a whole flood of memories coming back and upsetting you. Not saying you have to do this forever, just until you feel ready!

One thing to bear in mind is the drink and dial stumbling block! You know when you have a few alcoholic drinks and you feel nostalgic or mad and you call your ex. Be careful you could regret it the next day!

Remember, time is a great healer. This book is here to provide you with some solutions that can help the healing process and give you the keys to un-lock your new life from the inside out.

Rushing into another relationship isn't always the answer either! While it may feel like exactly what you need right now, it is not fair on you or the other person if you are not emotionally available. You don't need any more drama!

Instead, enjoy your single life. Pleasing yourself without trying to please others is a great place to be! Your life and happiness is in your control. You are the master of your own ship.

At this important time in your life it is a good idea to make sure all your paperwork is in order like the mortgage, car, health care, travel insurance, house insurance and life insurance. By letting these items slip your attention you could end up in a mess and potentially lose a lot of money.

If you are finding it hard to talk to anyone close to you, there are other professional people available.

Have a look at these organizations:-

www.beyondblue.org

www.relationshipsaustralia.com.au

It would be good to try and avoid joining any negative groups that focus on your past. Look at the name of the organisation and research it. Is it something that you feel you can benefit from?

Perhaps give them a call and have a chat. If you have a feeling that perhaps it is not right for you, listen to your gut. There are plenty of great groups out there and the ones you should be a part of will help you overcome your past and focus on your future.

When you think you are ready to start dating again, it is important to spend some time thinking about what you want from your next relationship and partner. This section is covered later on in the book under dating again.

In the meantime, relax enjoy your time as a single man again and the exciting journey that is ahead for you.

When you are focused on the positive, there will come a point in your life when you will feel you are ready to meet new people. If you haven't been on the dating scene for years, you will quickly realize the dating scene has changed.

21st Century Dating

For men, dating women in 2010's is different to dating the 1980s and 90s.

In the 1980s, you would have either met you date through friends, work or at a pub and have asked her out in person. On the evening you would have driven to pick up your date, and then take her for dinner, later perhaps, dancing at a disco. The whole evening would be planned out and even if there was no chemistry between you, the night would still have gone ahead out of an old-fashioned thing called – politeness. You would have dropped her back home ending the evening on a plutonic note, or if you were interested asked for a second date.

Today things have changed. With the rise in popularity of Internet dating, there are over 1.3 million singles on just one of the most popular on-line dating sites looking for love in Australia alone.

Most people don't meet in person before agreeing to go on a date. In fact many of them have not had a phone conversation, basing a meeting on a photo, on-line profile, emails and texts.

The term date has been replaced with a coffee or a drink and is treated casually as an opportunity to assess if you would like to spend more time with that person and perhaps go on a proper date.

Today women would rarely agree to be picked up by a man from their home, rather choosing to meet at a location where there will be other people such as a bar or café.

When it comes to communication, texting or emailing to make arrangements for a meeting is now the socially acceptable.

Dating after separation is a different ball game. You have grown older, your morals and expectations have changed. You are now more cautious and have learned about relationships from your own personal experiences. You hopefully have gained a better insight in the type of person who suits you, your personality and your life goals.

There is also the likelihood the next woman you date will have also have at least one major relationship break up in her past. However, this is not an excuse to compare war stories on your first, second or even third date. This topic is covered later on in the book.

The Single Man's Manual is your own personalised guide and plan to starting over. Designed to help you focus on getting yourself to a better position where you make the right decisions about what you want and where you want to go in your life.

Now is a great time to start writing out your hopes, fears, goals and things you would like to achieve in the future.

Take a pen and put some of your initial thoughts on paper. They always take on new meaning when they are out of your head and written down.

The first step in your journey is your confidence.

The Cycle of Confidence

1. When you work on yourself, you feel better from the inside, which in turn makes you feel good most of the time.

2. You are more attractive to the opposite sex as you exude an X factor that is magnetic.

3. When you get knock-backs, you simply say "So what?" and go back to feeling good about yourself.

 Write down a minimum of three areas that you would change in your life if you had more confidence. These can be small like wearing different clothes or huge experiences like climbing Mount Everest.

It is good to be open to change and learn to enjoy your own company. Don't just sit in front of the TV like a couch potato or develop an obsession with computer games.

People who enjoy their own company have calming energy - they exude confidence. Throughout this book, you will learn about the importance of confidence and how powerful it can be in every aspect of your life.

Be realistic!

Change is not always easy. However change is often the best thing you can do for yourself! Try not to change too many parts of your life at once, as it can be overwhelming. It is good to take small steps.

Soon enough, changing areas of your life will become natural to you.

Welcome to your new world!!

Congratulations on taking the first step.

You have probably have had a rough time over the past few months or even years in your previous relationship. Your job may have suffered along with your family connections, your health; maybe even your waistline has seen better days!

The past is in your past. You can't change what happened. Now is a good time to focus your energy and look forward to your new life. Understand that from this point in your life, anything is possible! You can create a new life, new friendships and new possibilities.

Now is the time to change. Your Time!

Welcome to A Single Man's Manual – 7 steps to help you change your life from the inside out! At the end of this book there is a 7 week program that you can print off which help you combine all the tips provided and give you a step by step plan to getting your life back on track.

Enjoy the journey and we wish you all the best.

Chapter Two

Confidence & Positive Mental Attitude

"I was always looking outside myself for strength and confidence, but it comes from within. It is there all the time"

Andre Gide 1869-1951

Most people see confidence as being about image, looks and personality. Confidence actually is about believing in yourself and your abilities. Confidence is self-assurance, an X Factor when you walk into a room and turn heads.

Confidence is how you hold yourself, your posture, holding your head high. Many believe that attractive people are confident, however usually it is confident people who are thought to be attractive. Examples of people today who are not attractive in the traditional sense yet because of their confidence women find them appealing- Russell Brand, Michael Cain and James Cagney.

Women find confident men attractive. It's as simple as that!

Confidence can't be purchased or transferred from one person to another. Many people aren't born with it and yet it comes more naturally to some people more than others.

Taking a look at the list you have written previously. What would you do if you had more confidence? Ask for more money in your job? Ask the woman you fancy at work out on a date? Take up a new business venture? Imagine you could flick a switch and you had more confidence, how great would that be?

The good news is you can learn how to be more confident yourself. You already have all the answers. Confidence is simply a state of mind

How To Get Confidence

 Write your "I'm good at... list"

Firstly, write a list of talents you know you are good at. This should include special skills that you are proud of. It can be something simple like how you are good at giving advice to your friends or that you are good at golf or how much people love your jokes!

Include anything and everything that you know about yourself, what you like and what makes you happy. Be honest, don't worry you don't have to show anybody!

You can look at these notes as your own personal résumé. Keep it handy and when you are feeling low, read through it. It will be an instant pick-me-up.

For future reference, it is also great to have a quick read through before you go for a job interview even on a first date.

Whatever you do don't take it with you!! !

Help Somebody Else

Often the best way you can make yourself feel better is to help somebody else. You could do chores for a neighbor or ring a friend who is going through a tough time. When you focus on another person it takes your mind off your own thoughts and one of the most rewarding joys in life is making somebody else smile.

Embrace Your Uniqueness

Everyone is different and that is something to celebrate. The world would be a boring place if every person were similar. Most people spend their life wishing they were something they are not or wishing they had something other than what they have already.

Confident people celebrate their individuality.

Tips To Make You Appear More Confident On The Outside

There are simple easy techniques you can apply immediately to make you appear more confident on the outside, while your inside is still catching up.

Hold Your Head High

Confident people have good posture. Keep your back straight square your shoulders puff out your chest slightly (stay relaxed – not like Puff Daddy!). Keep your chin up and your eyes forward.

Practice this the next time you walk into a room full of people. Have a look at their reaction to you, especially the women in the room! You will be noticed!

One tip to try is act like you own bar or club, any place that you are entering – act like the owner!

Smile And The World Smiles With You!

Make a concerted effort to smile and smile often. Smiling makes you appear warm, friendly, approachable and above all, confident! If smiling is too much right now then simply relax the muscles of your face, which will make you appear calm.

Have a look at yourself in the mirror now and make sure that you do not have a nervous or uptight expression on your face. If you do, you will give the impression to others that you are not happy, angry or worried about something that makes you less approachable to others.

The Eye Contact Confidence Technique

Try walking down the street or sitting in a cafe. Make eye contact with a stranger, smile and hold it for a couple of seconds.

Practice this at least once a day.

You may feel uncomfortable at first. However, after some time it will become easier and fun. People who can make and hold eye contact have an air of confidence about them, which is attractive, especially to women.

Internal Confidence Tools To Make You Feel More Confident

Number 1 Rule, "Do not take it personally"

This is easier said than done. Nobody likes to be criticised. Try not to take comments personally. People are entitled to their opinions and will make judgments on you, at you and about you, all your life. It's just human nature.

If somebody says something negative to you thank him or her for his or her opinion and keep on looking forward.

The cliché "like water off a ducks back" attitude works best. Confident people don't take other people's opinions personally. They never own another person's emotions or thoughts. They evaluate how they feel about a certain situation then decide if they want to take notice of it or not.

On the flip side of this, learn how to accept compliments. Don't shrug them off, take them on board and say "thank you" and smile.

Just Do It! - Take the Nike approach!

It is surprising just how powerful a small action can be towards your goals. One task completed breaks the cycle of procrastination. Whether it is sending an email to an old friend or doing a spring-clean of your desk or home. Small or large, action brings with it confidence, enthusiasm, excitement and the knowledge that other things can be done as well.

Write three tasks that you can do now to move you forward into action.

Fake It Until You Make It

Even if you don't feel it, just acting confidently can help you towards naturally feeling better about yourself. Remember to not care about what others think of you. Other people's opinions are just their opinions – nothing else!!

You Should Only Care About How You Feel About Yourself!

Don't compare yourself to other people. Know yourself and what you expect from your life and focus on those goals. You are your thoughts. Concentrate on what you want and know you can achieve anything.

Watch Your Words

Try to speak positively as much as you can. Should you catch yourself saying anything negative about yourself, replace it with a positive comment. There are always going to be people out there who will say negative comments about you, learn to rise above them and remember the good points that people have said about you, they will out-weigh the bad, every time!

It's simple - think good thoughts about yourself.

The best key factor in being confident is to have a positive mental attitude.

"It's A State Of Mind!"

The mind is an amazing instrument. When you learn to make use of your minds potential it's like having a power tool that is much faster, easier, and more efficient than doing the same job by your hands.

Your mind affects the world around you because your thoughts have energy. The universe is made up of energy. Your mind influences the world through your thoughts, feelings, and actions in obvious and subtle ways.

To state it simply: Happy thoughts equal a happy world.

It takes the same amount of energy to be happy, as it is to be sad so why not be happy?

When you dwell on the negative areas of your life and compare your failings to another's you can become depressed and discouraged.

Deciding to have a positive mental attitude will improve your outlook on life.

Think about these points below to retrain your thoughts.

Live For You

If you constantly try to be the person that other people want, you are cheating yourself out of your own dreams. Look at what you want out of your life and plan your daily routine to include at least one or two elements that bring your goals closer.

You have been a person that your partner has wanted to you be for the last few years. Now it is time to think who you want to be as a single entity and not as part of a romantic partnership.

For example: - What would you like your life to look like 6 months from now?

What do you want out of your life?

Understand

You can't control everything in your life. However you can control your reaction to them.

For example: - If you dislike your job and have a boss who is a pain in the butt, his poor behavior can only upset you if you allow it to. You can always find the funny side of his actions these will make for great stories and jokes to entertain your friends and colleagues.

Leaving Things Behind

Leave your work at the office. When you step outside after a trying days work, tell yourself that you have tomorrow to deal with the problems.

Instead of running to the nearest pub for a drink, there are plenty of ways you can relax. You can do one or all of the below. They will help you to change your state of mind.

1. Have a shower
2. Wear casual clothes in the house not your suit
3. Put some of your favorite music on
4. Go for a walk or run
5. Phone a friend and have a chat about their day instead
6. Go to the gym
7. Meditate
8. Have a massage

Having a positive mental attitude can affect not just yourself but everybody around you as well.

A positive attitude will benefit your mental and physical health. Imagine walking into a room and radiating positive energy. What great signals it would give off to the rest of the people in the room?

Exercise

Regular exercise will not only improve your health, it will help motivate you in other areas of your life and increase your energy levels. When you have a good work out you release a natural hormone called endorphins. Endorphins make you feel good for many hours.

Later in the book there is a whole section on the benefits of exercise.

Energy

To have the enough energy and drive to complete a task, a positive attitude is essential.

Putting your head down and grinding through a difficult situation with a positive outlook is much more rewarding than simply giving up!

Having A Sense Of Direction

Looking at the positive side of life will take you far. If you focus on the positives in life then you will get positive results.

Respect those with positive attitudes. Being positive says you believe in you, that you can achieve success, which you can!

Using positive language in your thoughts will give you the power to become the better person you want to be.

Now that you have learned how to be more confident and created a positive mental attitude, it is time to apply it to some new activities.

Chapter Three

Hobbies, Interests & Arts & Culture

"Today is life-the only life you are sure of. Make the most of today. Get interested in something. Shake yourself awake. Develop a hobby. Let the winds of enthusiasm sweep through you. Live today with gusto."
Dale Carnagie

Getting involved with hobbies, interests and Arts & Culture can occupy your newly acquired spare time. They can also provide the opportunity to meet new people. There is more to Arts & Culture than ballet or opera so keep an open mind!

Learning something new is always good for keeping your mind alert and active, keeping a long-term interest in an activity gives you a sense of achievement.

A hobby is a spare-time recreational pursuit, something you do for fun that you do for yourself.

Having a hobby will also help you become a more interesting, well-rounded person. It gives you something else to talk about with your friends, colleagues and your future dates!!

Remember this when you are deciding which one you want to do - conversations about stamp-collecting normally could put a person to sleep!

Think of a hobby that might interest you. It might be something that you always wished you had time to explore or perhaps your previous partner did not approve of you pursuing.

What a great time to now either get back into that hobby or take one up.

The best new hobby to pick would be a team sport. Is there a sport or activity that you would love to learn? This is a great way to meet new people, even potential dates. Sports that were historically male dominated now attract many women like golf, football, and skydiving.

At the end of this chapter there is a sample list of hobbies and sports.

What hobbies and interests did you once have that you would like to do again?

What hobbies have you not done before that you would like to try?

Here are a few points to consider when taking up a new interest.

How much will it cost and how much time it would take to learn and play?

Do you have the funds available for this?

Would you have the patience it would take to learn to play or train for any of these sports?

Would you rather play a team sport or an individual sport?

Are there are friends or family members who already have equipment you can use? Ask them about their experiences and listen to their suggestions.

Maybe take up something outdoors like fishing, hiking, water-skiing or cycling. Being outdoors and getting fresh air will make you feel great.

If after some time you start to enjoy your new pastime, then consider joining a club. Then you will meet new people with a common interest.

Search the Internet or visit a local library/community centre for more information.

Where possible pick a hobby that is close to your work or home so you don't add extra travelling time to your day as this can cause unnecessary stress in your life. The last thing you want right now is another chore that makes your eyes roll when you think about it, like ironing!! !

Make sure your hobby will not take away the time you need to spend with your family and friends. Ask them to come and watch you play or to take it up with you.

Get proper instructions on how to get the most out of your hobby and don't try to do anything difficult unless you have had proper training. This especially when it comes to the contact sports, best to avoid getting a black eye!

Have patience with your new hobby. Practice makes perfect. Enjoy the process and give yourself time to learn.

Now whilst on the topic of hobbies, sitting at the pokies and gambling is not a hobby. It can become an obsession and cost you a lot of money. Keep balance and perspective.

Once you have found your new hobby make sure to update your on-line social profile with it, discussed later on in the book.

Hobbies

    Cooking

    Creating Art like drawing, sculpture, woodwork

    Photography

    DIY, building

    Gardening

    Coaching sport teams

    Mentoring

    Home brewing

    Chess / Backgammon / Drafts

Here is a list of some sports to think about – you can always have a look on-line for more: -

Archery	Car Racing
Baseball	Basketball
Boating	Boxing
Road Cycling	Mountain Biking
Sailing	Bowling
Mountain Climbing	Cricket
Bunge jumping	Para Sailing
Parachuting	Fishing
Football	Rugby Union
Rugby League	Golf
Hockey	Horse Riding
Billiards	Hunting
Martial Arts	Motor Cycling
Water Polo	Horse Polo
Running	Triathlons
Snow Skiing	Soccer
Water-Skiing	Surfing
Swimming	Squash/Tennis

Arts & Culture

Now before you think you have to wear a cravat and smoke a pipe to be interested in Arts & Culture let's take a look at what it is all about today. You will be surprised at what it covers.

Arts & Culture includes the following interests, Design Arts, Film, Music, Literature, Performing Arts and Visual Arts.

Design Arts
- Advertising
- Architecture
- Industrial & Interior Design
- Fashion & Furniture Design
- Film
- Animation
- Documentaries
- Experimental Film
- Hollywood Film
- Indi & International Films
- Television

Music
- Blues / Jazz
- Opera
- Classical
- Dance / Trance / Electronic
- Country
- Folk
- Pop
- Rhythm & Blues
- Rock
- Hip Hop / Rap

Literature
- Digital Writing
- Fiction
- Non-Fiction
- Poetry

Performing Arts
- Ballet
- Comedy
- Jazz & Tap Dance
- Modern & Contemporary Arts
- Theatre

Visual Arts

- Conceptual Art
- Digital Art
- Drawing
- Painting
- Photography
- Print Making
- Sculpture

So as you can see Arts & Culture covers many areas of interest.

This list can also provide you with a great source of date suggestions when you are asking somebody out!

Where can you find a list of all that is going on in your city?

Well the best place to start would be the papers then the next place would be to have a look on-line.

You will impress a woman if you ask her what she is interested in and then, when the time is right, make plans to take her to that event. Definite brownie points!

Chapter Four

Social Interaction

"The past is behind, learn from it. The future is ahead, prepare for it. The present is here, live it."
                    Thomas S. Monson

As the years progress people lose contact with friends and colleagues. Life is busy you can drift apart as your circumstances change thus becoming more difficult to keep in touch. It's no big deal, it happens to most people. The great news is today there are many ways to reconnect with the people you would like to be back in touch with.

Re-connecting With Positive Friends

It is a good idea to surround yourself with people who are going to support you. Facebook and other social networking websites like twitter can reconnect you with old friends you have lost touch with.

Have a think about who you have lost touch with and you would like to reach out to again?

How To Find Friends That You Have Lost Touch With

Google search is a great tool to start with.

For example, let's say you are looking for James King from the Northern Beaches area of Sydney.

Take a look on free people search engines. These websites can be of use to provide you with basic information that you may not be able get elsewhere on the web.

On websites such as Facebook you will find that one friend leads to another.

There are websites specific to Australians. One is called OzReunion. Through their service you can search for people from school, sports clubs, family and friends classifications.

When it comes to re connecting with old contacts do your best to be considerate and polite. Focus on learning about how they have been and not on what you need from them.

Look back through the last communication you had with them. How did you leave it? This update will come in useful when you are trying to start up a conversation.

Keep in mind that friendship building is important for everybody and most people will be pleasantly surprised by your effort. Imagine how great you will feel when you start talking to that person again.

Offer them times to get together, arranging to meet near somebody's workplace can make it easier for both of you.

The purpose of meeting up again is not to ask them for something, so remember this when you are getting in touch. If you need them for a specific favour, then you need wait until you find out more about them and their lives before asking for anything back. It might not be the right time!

Now for couple of points to consider when contemplating contacting an old flame!

Where are they in their lives at this moment in time?

Would getting back in touch with them cause upset or could it enhance where you left things off?

Remember, an ex is an ex and you ended for a reason. Just because they come up as a suggested friend in Facebook does not act as an open door to re-kindle old embers! As mentioned earlier in the book drinking and dialing!! A new point to consider in today's world is having one too many drinks and then going on-line. Often when something is written down it is more cringe worthy the next morning!

Keep in mind the concept of beer-goggles - making somebody look more attractive is not exclusive to real life and applies when you are looking at profiles on the Internet.

Once you are back in touch, find out when the persons birthday or anniversary is. Even if you were only contacting them once a year, it will mean a lot that you remembered.

Whilst on the topic of special occasions, in many relationships the woman has kept a note of all the special family and friends' events in your life. Organising presents and sending cards so now it is up to you to remember.

Now is a great time to collect all the birthday/anniversary information from your family and friends. Put them in your on-line calendar or your diary, placing a reminder a week before so you time to remember.

Write down a list of family and friends birthdays including special events like anniversaries you would like to remember so you can either drop them a line, send them a card or even a present.

Being Social Again

Sometimes in the weeks and months after a break up, the last thing you want to do is meet new people. If you can push yourself to go out to new social events, even if it is just for one hour in the beginning, you will be surprised how good it will make you feel.

New coping skills may be required to get you over the nervous feelings you may have about new social interactions. If so, go back to confidence chapter if you like and read it again.

Here are some tips to help you get over any nerves you have about meeting new people:

Smile, Relax And Make Eye Contact.

Remember, when chatting to someone the other person might be more nervous than you are. By coming over relaxed, smiling and making eye contact, you will appear on the outside more confident which will put the other person at ease.

When starting conversations with a stranger, it is good to talk about general topics of what is going on in the world. A good tip before you go to a social event is to watch the news or a current affair show. Even a quick scan through the newspapers or on-line news websites can help if you are in a hurry.

Be Yourself And Have A Good Time.

Be aware of your appearance and what your style says about you. Dressing well and having good hygiene is necessary for making a good impression. Knowing that you look good will make you feel good too.

It would be great if you could stretch yourself to accept invitations to events that you would not have usually done when you were in a relationship.

A good tip is not to use alcohol or drugs for some Dutch courage to get you through the evening! Turning up drunk is never going to impress anybody!

Chapter Five

Fitness

'To feel fit as a fiddle you must tone down your middle'
Unknown

A man who is physically fit has a toned and trim body. They take pride in their appearance and take care of themselves. They know how important it is to have regular exercise and lead a healthy lifestyle, which includes eating well, drinking alcohol in moderation and not smoking.

The above is one of the official definitions to define fitness. If you are physically fit, you are free from illness and able to function efficiently and effectively to enjoy leisure and to cope with emergencies.

Health-related parts of physical fitness include body composition, cardiovascular fitness, flexibility, muscular endurance and muscle strength. Skill-related components include agility, balance, co-ordination, power, reaction time, and speed.

All sounds a little serious! Most women these days try to lead a healthy lifestyle therefore are drawn towards partners who enjoy keeping themselves fit. It goes back to the caveman days, where the hunter was always fit!

However this doesn't mean going to the gym 24/7 and trying to look like a Fabio or Hulk Hogan! Just looking after your physic a little! Let's face it being a bit trimmer will make you feel better, look more attractive and possibly make you perform a bit better in the bedroom!

Fitness means being able to perform many different types of physical activities. It also means having the energy and strength to feel as good as possible. Getting more fit, even a little bit, can also improve your health, which will make you feel better by giving you more confidence and making you more attractive to women.

This topic focuses on health-related fitness, will help you feel better and help lower your risk of certain diseases. By making small changes in your daily lifestyle will help you improve your fitness. Doing a little exercise gives you a healthy glow which women love!

Get Active - Healthy Body, Healthy Mind

Fitness helps you feel better and have more energy for work and leisure time. When you are fit and active your body and mind are working at their best.

When you stay active and fit, you burn off more calories even when you are resting. Imagine how good that would feel!! Being fit allows you do more physical activity and allows you exercise harder without as much effort.

Fitness is good for your heart, lungs, bones, and joints. Being fit lowers your risk of heart attack, diabetes, and high blood pressure, even, some cancers. It can also help you sleep, handle stress and keep your mind sharp.

If you find yourself getting out of breath when doing simple things like running to catch a bus, or climbing a flight of stairs, it is time to improve your fitness levels.

Like discussed earlier in the book about taking up new hobbies or sports, joining a new team perhaps rugby, touch football or a soccer team will help you improve your health as well as making new friends and widening your social circle. You never know who you might meet!

Include Physical Activity Into Your Daily Routine

One of the reasons you may be out of shape is because you don't regularly challenge your body to do anything out of its comfort zone. If you are ready to add a little more physical exercise into your life, here are some ways to get you started.

You can simply add physical activity to part of your daily routine. Try using the stairs more often, walking to and from work or to the local shops. It is advisable to consult your doctor before you start an exercise regime, especially if you have health issues.

If you are not a morning person, don't pretend to be, after work on an evening is fine. It is a well-known fact that fat loss is an all day process. So imagine how good it would feel to be sitting at work all day knowing the fat is melting off you!

Now if you know you need a kick up the butt perhaps get one of your mates to be your fitness buddy? This can help you to get motivated and make exercise more fun. You are less likely to let your mate down and more likely to get those kilos off!

If you want a more regular exercise routine consider joining a fitness centre. Through the centre you can organise a personal trainer who will create a specific program tailored to you and your goals.

Your local community centre usually offers different fitness activities, adventures and courses. Both of these areas are great places to meet new people.

By varying your routine, perhaps the gym one day, footy the next, you will have a greater chance of getting in shape, feeling great and beating the boredom.

Now for some technical jargon to explain the different exercise regimes!

Aerobic

Aerobic exercise involves or improves oxygen consumption into the body. To get the best results a session would involve a warming up period followed by at least 20 minutes of moderate to intense exercise involving large muscle groups with a cooling down period at the end.

Anaerobic

Anaerobic exercise triggers anaerobic metabolism. Athletes use this technique; in non-endurance sports, to promote strength, speed and power and by body builders to build muscle mass. It involves muscular effort in short bursts followed by rest such as wind sprints or weight -lifting.

To help you succeed in your exercise program, it's good to schedule workouts into your calendar and stick to them. This makes it easier to remember and to build your day around them. Treat them as proper appointments and in a few weeks it will become part of your normal life routine.

It is important to remember it takes about eight weeks to see any significant results that will last. Remember, you can't undo years of neglect in one week!

If you are starting to gain weight, don't worry! Muscle weighs three times more than fat!

If you are keeping on track, you will be building more muscle. You can check this by recording your body measurements, noticing the fit of your clothes as your body becomes firmer and toned.

There is nothing like putting a spring in your step in a morning when you put on your jeans and they feel baggy.

Another way to keep a check on how you are going is to keep a record your BMI Body Mass Index. Go on-line and enter your height and weight into a body mass calculator. This will tell you if you are of the right weight or not and if not where you should be. Body Mass Index is just as important as weight loss.

You don't have to be on the go 24/7. It is important to get some beauty sleep somewhere down the line. Your body will tell you how many hours you will need, let it!

Doctors just aren't there when you are on your deaths-door. It's good to have regular check-ups. Today most doctors offer a complete head-to-toe body health check that scans all aspects of your body, bloods, liver and kidney functions. If you have one of these done every year, you build up a comprehensive profile of your health status and can make any changes as you need to. Prevention is better than cure!

Once you have reached your desired fitness, you will feel great! Continue to do what you are you don't want to be falling back down the slippery slope!

Wellness Is A Lifestyle!

Write down what goals you want to achieve and by when, for example

How much would you like to weigh in 3 months time?

How often would you like exercise every week?

How far would you like to run in one month's time?

Be realistic and once you have achieved them reward yourself.

Make A Contract With Yourself And Sign It.

My Fitness Contract

19th Nov 2009

I, John Smith, Agree to take up or continue
the following exercise regime every week:

1. An Hour of Running x 2
2. Swim 100 lengths x 1
3. Do 1 hour of Weights at the Gym x 1
4. Play Basketball once per week

In the next 6 months my desired weight is 90 kilos!

Signed:

Writing something like this will help you remember why you want to get fit. It is difficult to start or continue with a fitness program if you don't really know why you are getting fit.

Review the reasons why you want to get fit as this will help to motivate you.

Fitness is lifestyle. By following some of the tips in this chapter will help you achieve your goals and have fun on the way.

Chapter Six

Nutrition

> 'You are what you eat'
>
> Gillian McKeith

When people are conscious of what they put into their bodies, they feel better. They tend to follow a healthy lifestyle, which includes fitness. They consume food and drink that is good for them, as they know the benefits of having a balanced diet makes them feel great.

The definition of nutrition is the science that studies the process by which humans acquire all the things necessary for them to live and grow. Nutrition focuses on the role of nutrients, which are defined as substances that the body cannot make on its own. This includes vitamins, minerals, and certain macromolecules.

So basically, nutrition consists of diet (what you take in) and metabolism (what happens to it after it enters your body). If you are going to eat crap then you are going to look like crap!

Nutrition also focuses on how diseases, conditions and problems can be prevented with a healthy diet. A poor diet can have a negative impact on health causing deficiency diseases such as scurvy and beriberi, health-threatening conditions like obesity and other such common diseases as cardiovascular disease, diabetes and osteoporosis.

There are many benefits of good healthy diet. As well as helping you keep a healthy weight, good nutrition is essential for the body to work for a lifetime. In fact the benefits of good nutrition can be found in physical and mental health because a healthy diet provides energy, promotes good sleep, gives the body what it needs to stay healthy and thus making will make you more attractive to the opposite sex! When you consider the benefits of good nutrition it's easier to eat healthy.

Energy

One big benefit of a healthy diet that you can see every day is your energy levels. Foods that contain excess sugar or that are high in fats can minimize your energy levels from day to day. Fats are slow to digest therefore don't provide your body with a steady source of energy.

Sugary foods can create fluctuations in blood sugar levels causing you to feel tired very shortly after eating. By eating a healthy diet you maintain your energy levels consistently throughout the day therefore you feel better and can perform better!

Self-Confidence

There have been many studies proven that junk food is not good for us. Yet many of us continue to indulge in them for emotional reasons even binge eating. Happiness has never been found at the bottom of a pizza box or cookie jar!

When you make the conscious choice to eat better and healthier you begin to feel better about yourself regardless of how quickly the weight comes off. Having the odd treat is fine and it tastes much better when it is not consumed with guilt!

Nobody likes to go out for a meal and have the other person pushing their peas around the plate with a fork! Calorie counting and no carbs after 2pm! Zzzzzzz !

Primary Food Groups

No single food contains all the nutrients needed for health, so you should try to eat a balanced diet. By choosing various foods from the five food groups you will get all the nutrients you need to stay healthy and active.

There are five main foods groups are:

Protein

Meat, poultry, fish, eggs, nuts and pulses such as beans, chickpeas and lentils are all included in this group. They are rich sources of protein, vitamins and minerals, especially iron and zinc. Meat protein helps the absorption of iron from vegetables and cereals.

Pulses such as peas, beans and lentils also contribute to fiber intake. By choosing leaner cuts of meat and using low-fat cooking techniques, you will help to reduce your total fat intake. Protein is essential for tissue growth and repair, immune system protection, vision and oxygen. One of the other major reasons is that it helps you feel fuller for longer.

Good Carbohydrates, Bread, Cereals and Potatoes

Bread, pasta, rice, cereals and potatoes are all part of this group. Carbohydrates should be the main part of a meal. In fact should be around one-third of food consumed. They are the main source of energy as well as providing vitamins, minerals and fiber.

These healthy carbohydrates (called complex crabs) contain naturally occurring sugars that the body can easily and slowly metabolise for balanced brain function, mood attitude and useful energy.

Naughty Carbohydrates

These include chocolate; cakes, cookies, sweets and anything made with refined sugar or flour or processed white rice.

Eat too many of these foods and you run the risk of mood swings. You may become depressed, angry and irritable. Excess bad carbohydrate residues are stored as fat in the body. If that is not enough, years of bad carbohydrate eating could also lead to diabetes.

Fruit and Vegetables

This group includes all fresh, frozen, canned, dried and juiced fruit and vegetables. They provide a wide range of valuable vitamins, minerals and fiber. It is recommended that you should eat at least 5 portions of fruit and vegetables a day.

Milk and Dairy Products

This group is a great source of protein, vitamins and minerals and they represent the richest source of calcium in your diet. You should choose low-fat versions such as semi skimmed or even skimmed milk, which contain just as much calcium, protein and minerals.

Consuming enough calcium to maintain and promote bone health is essential. You can avoid many bone conditions that may develop later in life by providing your body with enough calcium in your diet.

Good Fats

Good fats on the other hand are essential in our diets. In this day and age of low-fat foods and fat-free diets have created a war against fats and in turn meant that many of us have become confused about the issue.

Good fat foods such as nuts, seeds and avocados are the healthiest option. These are the good fats are important and necessary for life itself. These fats help you to metabolise fat.

Flax seeds, sunflower seeds, sea vegetables, fish and avocados are good examples of these essential thinning fats.

Naughty Fats Oils and Sugar

This group provides energy but they don't offer much nutritional value. They are not essential for a healthy diet. High bad-fat diets raise blood pressure and cholesterol levels. By avoiding foods that are high in unsaturated fats and cholesterol you can lower your chance of heart disease and possible failure in later life.

Medical research has proved that certain foods do increase the risk of heart disease and there is a direct link to unsaturated fats and cholesterol. The heart is the essential core of our bodies. By avoiding foods that contain these heart unhealthy substances you can ensure your heart will perform properly for years to come.

Bad fats can interfere with blood sugar levels and cause liver stagnation, which can lead to depression and weight gain. Bad fats do add variety and choice and most of us eat too much of this group, so try to limit your intake on take outs, fry ups and trans fat foods.

Fluid

Water is your body's principal chemical component making up around 60 percent of your body weight. Every system in your body depends on water.

Water flushes toxins out of vital organs, carries nutrients to your cells and provides a moist environment for ear, nose and throat tissues. Water is great for your skin, giving you that sexy healthy glow.

Lack of water can lead to dehydration, a condition that occurs when you don't have enough water in your body to carry out normal functions. Even mild dehydration can drain your energy and make you tired and sick.

The Institute of Medicine advises that men consume roughly 2 liters (about 13 cups) per day. Your intake of some foods will help provide some of the water your body requires on a daily basis.

So How Do You Start Eating More Healthily?

The good news is that you do not have to sacrifice taste or flavour to have a healthy diet. Small changes to recipes can make a big difference to your overall nutrition.

One of the easiest ways you can improve your lifestyle is to swap out unhealthy ingredients for more wholesome ones. Here are some simple steps that you can take.

Fat

Many recipes need oil or butter to help with the cooking process. Avoid lard or butter as much as possible. Instead, use low-fat olive or vegetable oils spreads where possible.

A non-stick cooking spray is the healthiest choice.

Not Too Many Eggs

Eggs are nutritious, however too many eggs do have a downside. Egg yolks contain lots of cholesterol that many people should avoid.

For healthy recipes that call for eggs, substitute two egg whites for one full egg.

Swap Yoghurt For Aioli

Yoghurt is a healthy and a low in fat alternative to mayonnaise. If you would like to make a recipe creamier or cool down something over-spiced, try using natural low-fat yoghurt.

Reduce Your Salt Intake

There are plenty more seasonings that are much better for you than salt. Garlic, herb mixtures, mustard, onions and celery can all be used as seasoning. See it as an opportunity to experience new tastes instead of using salt for everything. You don't have to eliminate salt, reducing your intake will be a big step towards your new healthy lifestyle.

Reduce Portion Size

If you halve the size of your food portions you'll be consuming half the calories - sounds simple right? Well in the beginning, you may feel hungry as your body adjusts to the new amount of food. In the early stages you can always go back for a small second help until you adjust. After a period of time your stomach will adapt and you will start to lose weight.

Expand Your Recipe List

Man cannot live on bread alone - or on that one dish that you can make like beans on toast.

Now that you are starting over, it's time to learn some new healthy dishes. Just two or three to start!

When you are cooking, make enough for four or six people. Then you can freeze the rest in individual plastic containers, left over from your old take-outs! Do this once or twice a week and you'll build up a stock of fresh healthy dishes in your freezer. Then on the nights that you come home late, you won't have to resort to a take away!

When you look at all the benefits of good nutrition, you will quickly realise that eating healthy and making healthy food choices results in a much better lifestyle. You will be reaping the benefits of good nutrition before you know it!

As you work on your fitness regime, start making new friends and learn to cook new dishes, you will start to feel better about yourself. Watch out for the compliments!

When you are feeling more adventurous you can check out cooking websites for new recipe. You may even think about signing up for a cookery class, another place to meet new women!

Women love guys who can relieve us from the stove!

Write five foods you are going to remove from your diet.

Write five foods you are going to include in your diet.

Write down what you would love to be able to cook to impress a potential date.

Chapter Seven

Taking Care of Yourself - Inside and Out

> 'I'll try anything once, twice if I like it, three times to make sure!'
>
> Mae West

In addition to fitness and nutrition there is the area of wellbeing. This covers areas from massage to spirituality. Might sound a bit hocus pocus to you right now, however try to keep an open mind and remember the point of this book is to make you feel better about yourself. Most of what is about to be discussed has been around for thousands of years.

Spa Treatments

Historically the domain of women, today it is very common to see men in spa resorts, salons and clubs. In fact in early Roman days, spas and public baths were the domain of men and soldiers, no women were allowed! So no need to feel like less of a man!

This chapter covers the different types of treatments available that can help you improve your mind, body and soul.

Massage

Massage, now what are you thinking? ! Take your mind out of the gutter, the clean version! Massage helps to relieve stress and improve the detoxification of the lymphatic system. It can also help improve the circulation of the blood.

Massage is a great relaxing, therapeutic treatment that has been around for thousands of years. In fact, the word "massage" comes from the Greek root "masso," which means to touch.

It is effective in managing pain for people who suffer from headaches, muscle spasms and arthritis. If you have a serious injury, it is best to consult your doctor.

The main types of massages are:

Swedish Massage

Swedish massage, no not done by a Scandinavian blonde chick! Is the most common massage offered and is the perfect place to start. The therapist will use a special oil to ensure smooth gliding strokes over the entire body. Other Swedish massage moves include kneading, friction and stretching.

Sports Massage

This massage was designed to help athletes prepare their bodies for peak performance or to recover.

Today a sports massage is useful for anybody with chronic pain, injury or range-of-motion issues. In this treatment the therapist will concentrate on a specific problem area for example, the neck or shoulders.

Deep Tissue Massage

This massage is aimed at the deeper tissues of the muscles also called connective tissue. It uses many of the same movements and techniques as in Swedish massage however the pressure will generally be more intense.

Deep tissue massage is a more focused type of massage as the therapist works to release muscle tension or knots.

Hot Stone Massage

This massage uses smooth stones that have been heated. The stones are usually basalt, a black rock from volcano's that absorbs heat well. The heat penetrates your muscles causing them to tighten and relax quickly.

Additional Therapies

Other than massage, there are many other forms of relaxation therapy to make you feel better inside and out.

Here are a few of the more popular ones:

Flotation Therapy

This is where you place your body into a state of total relaxation. It happens in a specially constructed bath. The water has salts and minerals dissolved in the bath to enable the body to float.

The flotation tank is a therapeutic area that breaks these habitual responses and reactions. It allows the mind and body to regenerate their natural energy without interference from the patterns of the outside world.

The flotation sometimes takes place in complete darkness and some establishments may play relaxation tapes or have a two-way microphone which allows for conversation with a practitioner.

Wraps

For this treatment your skin is given a body brush or exfoliation with sea salt, then you are completely covered in either mud or seaweed paste. You are then wrapped in foil and given an electric blanket to keep you warm.

This is relaxing and you could easily to nod off. Afterwards the paste or mud is washed off you followed by a light massage. When you get up you feel more relaxed and lighter.

All these treatments will put a spring in your step allow your skin to glow that women love.

Have a look on-line for salons and spas that specialise in treatments for men.

Write down a few treatments that you fancy having. Make a promise to yourself to have one new spa treatment experience in the next month.

Meditation

Now there is no need to shave your head and buy an orange robe! Though meditation is recognised as a primarily spiritual practice, it also has many health benefits. More women tend to meditate than men so it could be a great way of meeting new people.

The Overall Benefits Of Meditation.

1. General health. When your mind focuses on a particular part of the body the blood flow to that part increases and cells receive more oxygen and other nutrients in abundance.

2. Improvement in concentration. Many sports professionals regularly employ meditation methods.

Studies have found a direct correlation between concentration exercises such as meditation has increased the performance levels of sports professionals.

Meditation strengthens the mind and is able to provide effective guidance to the physical body to perform better.

So for people with high blood pressure, mediation could help to bring it back to normal. It also reduces the likelihood of anxiety attacks by lowering the levels of blood lactate.

Meditation decreases muscle tension (any pain due to tension) and headaches. It builds self-confidence and increases serotonin production that influences mood and behavior. Low levels of serotonin are linked with depression, obesity, insomnia and headaches.

Meditation also helps with chronic diseases such as allergies and arthritis by enhancing the immune system. Research has revealed that meditation increases activity of "natural-killer cells" which kill bacteria and cancer cells.

Different Types of Meditation

There are many types of meditation. To get you started, here are 3 types you can try.

1. Breath Watching.

Can meditating be as simple as paying attention to your breath for a few minutes? You bet! Relax in whatever position works best for you, close your eyes and start to pay attention to your breathing.

Breathing through your nose gets your diaphragm involved and gets oxygen all the way to the bottom of your lungs. As your mind wanders simply refocus your attention on the air going in and out of your nose.

Just do this for several minutes, or longer as you get used to it.

2. An Empty Mind Meditation

Meditating can create an "awareness without object," an emptying of all thoughts from your mind. The techniques for doing this involve sitting still often in a "full lotus" or cross-legged position and letting the mind go silent. Initially, it can be difficult since any effort seems to cause more business in the mind.

3. Walking Meditations.

This one gets the body involved. It can be outside or simply as a back and forth pacing in a room. Pay attention to the movement of your legs and breathing and body as you walk and to the feeling of your feet contacting the ground.

When your mind wanders just keep bringing it back to the process of walking and breathing. Meditating outside in this way can be difficult because of the distractions. If you do it outside, find a quiet place with level ground.

There are many other meditations you can try. Each type has its own advantages and effects. You may find that at different times and for different purposes you want to use several different types of meditation. Try them out and see what works for you.

Linked strongly with meditation has been yoga. Straight away it is easy to think this is not for you however read on!

Yoga

Yoga is not just for women! It's a healing system of theory and practice. A combination of breathing exercises, physical postures and mediation that has been practiced for more than 5000 years. There are many benefits of yoga. It's not just you men who like women to be flexible in the bedroom!

The Feel Good Factor of Yoga

1. Improved posture, increased intake of oxygen and enhanced functioning of the respiratory, digestive, endocrine, reproductive and elimination systems.

2. Calming the mind, attuning us to the environment and reduced insomnia caused by your mind working overtime.

Yoga is recommended for people in competitive, stressful working environments, for those who suffer from headaches, back and shoulder aches, allergies, and asthma and for anyone over the age of 40.

Yoga also works to unite the split between the mind and the body.

Personal Grooming

'You are your greatest asset. Put your time, effort and money into training, grooming, and encouraging your greatest asset.'
Tom Hopkins

Appearances are so important in the world in which you live today. Whether you like or not, women make judgment on the way you look. And this first impression can reflect how you are seen as a person. It may sound shallow, unfortunately that's just the way it is!

Now you don't have to go as far as having an extreme makeover or a face-lift. All you have to do is take a little more care in yourself.

Here are some tips to help men create a great impression.

Skin

The skin is the largest organ in the body and is subject to the same laws as all your organs. If your skin is mistreated for long enough it will make you look 10 years older and who wants that?

Modern life adds stress on your body. Your skin is the first contact for air pollution, chemicals in water and air-conditioning.

The health of your skin is also affected by what you eat and drink. For example, caffeine-high products, smoking, foods high in fat/sugar and drinking alcohol all add stress to your skin. And as for exposing your skin to too much sun this can create a look of crocodile hide!

By leading a healthier lifestyle, as discussed in the earlier chapters, you can have a much healthier glow on the inside, which will show on the outside. This in turn will make you look younger and more appealing to the opposite sex.

How To Take Care of Your Skin

When you jump in the shower, the soap or shower gel that you use on your body is not necessarily the best for the skin on your face. Now is a good time to invest in a facial cleanser as these are designed to clean deep into the layers of the skin and remove dirt and toxins.

With the harsh Australian sun even twenty minutes outside can damage your skin. It is best to use an oil-free facial moisturizer with an SPF30 every day to hydrate the skin and protect from sun damage.

Use the products appropriate for your skin type. Visit a skin care counter to get information on the men's lines available. For severe acne, consult a dermatologist.

Shaving

Now when it comes to shaving, there are two schools of thought from the female camp. The shaven look and the rugged look! The clean-shaven look is attractive and kissable. However, if you are going to keep up with this look, watch your stubble growing back in after a day or so, as we want to have skin left on our chin!

The rugged look, can incredibly sexy and women are less likely to get beard rash! Think of Russell Crow in Gladiator!

Man-scaping

Man-scaping, now what is all that about? More and more women these days are attracted to men who pay attention to the hair on their bodies, yes! All over your body! It is called it "Man-scaping". This is when a guy trims or shaves his body hair to appear neat and groomed. Believe it or not it is becoming the norm. It can also make certain parts of your body appear larger!

If you have hairy back, you might want to consider waxing or laser treatment for a long-term removal. If you have really hairy chest and armpits, thin them with regular trimmings with clippers.

It is also important to keep an eye on the extra hair that grows in your ears and up your nose. Not to mention, as you get older, your eyebrows seem to spurt extra hair and in extreme cases causing a mono-brow. This is never an attractive look - only for clingon's!

Hair (on your head)

You may have been going to your barber for years and would never think about going to a hairdressing salon.

Perhaps invest in an appointment with a good hairdresser (that doesn't mean they have to be expensive) and ask for advice on what styles would suit your face shape, age and hair color and quality. Make sure the style of haircut you choose is appropriate to the look you are trying to achieve.

You can also look in magazines for hairstyles that you like. Collect a few pictures and bring them to the hairdresser.

Once you have a good styled cut, it is much easier to keep your hair looking good.

Hair products for men have also increased in number and quality in recent years. Use a good shampoo and conditioner as often as needed to keep your hair looking shiny and clean.

Choose from the wide range of hair grooming products on the market to keep your hair styled and neat throughout the day.

Many men dye their hair either to hide graying hair or to create a fun, modern look. Make sure you use well-known brands or have it done at a salon to avoid problems. Women can spot that orange or purple glow of a 7-11 home brand dye job from a mile off!

Showering

Always make sure to take regular showers and wash yourself well, especially before a hot date! Use antibacterial shower products and please wear deodorant. Condition your hair and apply a body spray or after-shave.

After Shave

This is another personal preference between women. Some prefer either lots of after-shave or none at all. However on an evening out it shows you have made a little more effort!

Next time you are out and about pop into your local chemist or department store and try a few out. Remember, each after-shave smells different on each person, so try it on your skin first and smell it in 5 minutes time when the scent has calmed down.

Dental Care And Fresh Breath

Make sure to visit the dentist twice a year for a check-up. If you don't take care of your teeth, cavities and gums you are going to get an unhealthy mouth and no one is going to want to kiss that!

Brush your teeth twice a day and floss. Remember, it is not the toothpaste that cleans your teeth; it's the mechanical action of the bristles in physical contact with the tooth surface that removes plaque.

Using dental floss or tiny inter-dental brushes that reach in between and under the contact points where your toothbrush can't are important to get rid of any bacteria building. Gum disease is linked to life-threatening illnesses such as heart disease, stroke, and diabetes.

Clean Hands And Finger Nails

There is nothing worse than meeting a man who has dirty fingers and finger nails. One of the first areas a woman looks at is a mans hands. It you are a tradesman then we will let you off, to a point. Scrub those hands! You will see now it is getting increasingly common today to find men in salons getting manicures and even pedicures. If you prefer to do it at home here are some pointers.

Soak in dishwashing liquid and warm water for about ten minutes. This softens the nail bed, loosens any dirt lodged under and around the nail and removes any little filing particles that might still be on your nails.

Use a soft flat nailbrush to scrub your nails as well as the skin on your hands.

Pumice also removes most stains that don't respond to regular soap and water or rubbing a lemon wedge over the discolored area.

Cut only nails with a cuticle scissors or trimmers do not cut the rim that protects the nail bed.

Then apply hand cream or lotion at this stage, if you like? It's ok; you don't have to tell your mates!

Pedicure

And finally... it is time to take care of your feet.

Looking your best isn't only for the women, nowadays! In the age of the metro sexual male, many men are making it a point to pay close attention to their grooming habits. That includes getting pedicures!

The same procedure applies to your feet as your hands. There is a great tool that has come onto the market for getting rid of the hard skin on the bottom of your feet. If is called a 'Ped-egg' and they are excellent, so be brave and get rid of that rough skin!

 Write down a minimum of three new areas you are going to address in your Personal Grooming area.

How To Dress

'Clothes and manners do not make a man, but when he is male, they will greatly improve his appearance'

> Henry Ward Breecher

Today there is more emphasis on men of all ages to look their best both professionally and personally. Confidence shines through when you look and feel your best!

It takes around 10 seconds for someone to make an impression of you when they first meet you. This impression is based upon your appearance.

Below is a breakdown of the key elements on how to dress to show you how you can make the best of your coloring and body type.

Color

Wearing the right color is an easy way for you to improve your image. The impact of color on mood is well understood by women however, what most men don't know is that color also impacts the way you look, your perceived age, attractiveness and confidence.

You can take years off your look or communicate greater confidence just by knowing the right colors to wear.

Firstly decide which colors best suit your skin tone. If you are unsure it may be worthwhile going to see a consultant at a department store.

A large department store will usually employ personal assistants to advise on their clothing ranges. Alternatively you can get in touch with personal stylists in your city. Meet up with a couple to see who really see "you" for you and that you connect with. Remember you have to feel comfortable with your new look.

A person is drawn to a particular color they like. It is important to hold up different shades against your face so you can see how the different tones change your look.

Wearing colors that suit you near to your face will enhance your skin and hair tone giving you an extra vibrant look. Wearing dark colors in potential problem areas will divert attention. If you feel uncomfortable, a great slimming down exercise can be to wear one color, preferably a darker color.

It will make the body appear as one unit and can make you appear taller and therefore slimmer.

Wear Clothes That Fit

If you wear the wrong size clothes you will look bigger than you are. Wearing clothes that are too tight will cause bulges. Wearing clothes that are too big for you add to your size and make you look larger.

Professional Dressing

In a business or corporate scenario first impressions are even more important.

A well dressed and well groomed professional will look like a highly trained individual and in turn earn the respect of their peers and prospective clients.

Suits

Single-breasted suits are more in fashion at the moment. A double-breasted suit should be worn for a more conservative situation.

Go for something neutral. These colors include grey, black, brown, beige or navy blue. A color that utilises pin stripes is also acceptable. This will add color and texture to a suit.

Always purchase a suit as a two-piece. Do not mix and match, you may already have a black pair of trousers however there are so many different fabrics and finishes. If you need a suit, buy a suit!

Suits will often not fit everyone straight off the rack. All body types are different so it is best to take the suit to a tailor for a better fit.

Shirts

It is best to wear a more traditional shirt made of either cotton or cotton-blend shirts with long sleeves and straight or button collars. Since the suit is of neutral color it will match up to any color shirt. For more conservative occasions wear a white shirt.

Ties

A tie should reach your belt buckle. The most professional way to wear a tie is the Windsor knot. A Windsor knot is thick, wide and triangular tie knot that projects confidence.

Silk ties are the best followed by polyester that looks like silk. A professional choice would be classic polka dot, paisley or repetitive patterns in dark colors.

Underwear

Ensure you know your size and style. In reality most women prefer men in fitted trunks no matter what your shape or size is, it's a safe bet and it works. Please don't wear them for days! Keep them clean and fresh. Check out magazines to see what is on offer these days.

Dress For Your Shape

The following information has been collated thanks to the famous Trinny and Susannah – "What not to wear".

MAN BOOBS

Do Wear

Vertical stripes on shirts - this will elongate your body making you look thinner.

Natural fabrics - they will be more comfortable and move naturally on your body.

Prints not plain – be careful of the types of prints you choose - not Hawaiian shirts.

Layered clothes. Choose vertical layering like a waistcoat over a t-shirt. Shirts with breast pockets.

Don't Wear

Shiny fabrics like football shirts - these will make you look bigger than you are.

Fine knit jumpers - this material will cling to your man boobs and make them look bigger.

High neck short- sleeved t-shirts - these again highlight your man boobs.

THIN

Do Wear

Logos on your shirts - these will help make you look bigger.

Short-sleeved shirts - these look good on your shape.

Skinny jeans - you are one of the few body shapes that can carry off these jeans. Hipster trousers are also flattering on your body shape.

Suit jackets – these give your body shape and structure making you looks bigger too.

Don't Wear

High waisted trousers - these will make you look too thin.

Contrasting colors - keep colors within the same tonal range. For example - blacks and grays are fine, do not wear black and white. Fat ties -will take over too much of
your body andlook comical.

Chunky Sweaters - will make you look out of proportion and your legs too skinny.

Horizontal stripes - can make your look too top-heavy and have matchstick legs.

TOP HEAVY

Do Wear

Bootleg trousers - these have a slight flare on the ends and they will help balance out your top half.

Long Scarves - these will help to give you a leaner look.

Fitted Jackets with two buttons - as they help give your shape some definition and shape.

One button knee-length coats - as they will give you a longer, leaner look.

Small pattern shirts and t-shirts - as they will help balance out your shape.

Don't Wear

Short-sleeved shirts - as they will make your body look bigger that it is.

Tapered trousers or skinny jeans - as they will make your top half look bigger.

Football shirts – they should only be worn when going to watch the football or in the privacy of your own home.

Shirts or Jumpers that are lighter than your trousers - keep your top half in darker colors, as this will make you look thinner

SHORT LEGS

Do Wear

The entire same color - like all black or all grey - this will make your body look in proportion and taller.

Vertical stripes on your shirts - as these will make you look taller too.

Flat-topped shoes - will lengthen your legs, rather than round topped shoes.

Match your shoes to your trousers - do not wear brown shoes with black trousers.

Layered tops, including shirt, waistcoat and a jacket - will take the focus to your top half and away from your legs.

Don't Wear

Contrasting colors - black top and pale trousers - this will divide your body in two and highlight your legs.

Tops that come halfway down your thighs - these will make your legs look even shorter.

Tops that are too short - wear tops just below your waist to give you proportion.

White trainers with jeans - they will make your legs look even shorter.

BEER BELLY

Do Wear

Loose T-shirts - they will create coverage for your stomach.

Low waisted jeans - will be more comfortable.

Scarves - (yes they are trendy for guys) can distract from your beer belly.

Darker colors - on top as they make you look thinner.

One continuous color - will help lengthen your shape and create a thinner looking body shape.

Don't Wear

Contrasting colors - these will draw attention to your middle area.

Three quarter length jackets - as they make your stomach area look bigger that it is.

Tops that are too long - will again make your beer belly look larger that it is.

Short tops - will show your tummy to the world.

Shoes that are a different color from your trousers - as they cut your legs off. Wearing shoes the same color as your trousers keeps your legs looking longer and leaner.

THICK NECK

Do Wear

Scarves - thin ones work best as they distract the eye from your neck area and down the body.

Unbuttoned shirts - not too many - one or two is fine as they create a v-neck shape on your body making your neck look thinner and longer.

V-necked jumpers or t-shirts - are good to create a better shape for your neck.

Big Collars on your shirts - help to create the illusion of a thinner neck.

Don't Wear

Small collars - they will only make your neck look bigger.

High round necks on jumpers or t-shirts - cut off the shape and make your neck look shorter than it is.

Shirts that are buttoned up to the top button - look too stuffy and do nothing to lengthen the shape of your neck.

Three buttoned jackets - create a line up towards your neck focusing again on its size.

Tight necklaces - will make you look like you are choking.

Your first task is to now head to your wardrobe and get rid of anything that does not suit you. Sell those clothes on eBay and use the money to go shopping for new clothes that work for you and your new life.

Write down your body type that you believe you are (check with a friend if you like)

List the clothes should you buy for your new look.

Chapter Eight

On-line World Social and Dating

'Dating should be less about matching outward circumstances, than meeting your inner necessity'
Anon

Most people today have an on-line profile of some description. Whether it is to make business contacts through professional networking sites like Linked-In or to stay connected with your friends and family on Facebook.

Different guidelines apply on different sites and a profile will vary depending upon the outcome. Here are a few points to help you get the most out of your profile.

Business Profile

For your business profile you only need one professional photo of yourself in your suit or work wear.

Keep interests and hobbies to a minimum. For example; 'I enjoy hiking or running.' There is no need to expand on a story.

The business profile will be what you do for work, how you do it and what you are looking to attract and achieve as well as what you offer in terms of support and service.

It is about creating yourself as an expert in your field and attracting potential clients. It can also help you find new work opportunities in future.

You can provide more value to your prospective clients by having a strong professional network to call upon if needed. Many networking websites help you do this easily.

Personal Profile

For your personal profile, you can have as many photos as you like. These sorts of websites are more casual and give an insight to your personal life. However, please remember to keep it respectful to yourself and others.

Be careful to read the directions for every one of these websites as sometimes when you think you are sending someone a personal message, you are in fact sending a public message. Remember, as the saying goes, don't send anything via email you wouldn't put on a billboard.

Personal websites are great for looking up old school friends or ex work colleagues. It can also help you connect with people with similar interests.

Write down a list of social networking sites that you would like to join.

Your Photograph - Why Do You Need A Decent Photograph?

In today's digital age there is important to have a decent photograph of yourself for on-line use.

Whether it is for professional use for example a business networking website like Linked-In or social networking website like Twitter or even catching up on Facebook, a decent photo is needed.

You have heard the saying your never get a second chance to make a first impression. From all the answers received during studies of Internet dating, it seems in the on-line world you only get a microsecond to make a good first impression! The first thing most people do is look at your profile photo.

The purpose of a profile photo is to take a photograph interesting enough that other people want to click on and find out more about you.

The Right Equipment

If you don't have a good digital camera or mobile phone with image capture settings, then it is time to treat yourself to a new one or both! You will be able to use it for more than just taking photos of yourself!

Experiment with the settings on the camera. For a range of tips for the beginner on how to take pictures, go to

www.dptutorial.com/photography-tips-for-beginners.

The Right Look

Wear clothes that suit you and that you feel most comfortable in. Make sure your hair is clean and tidy. You want to be looking your best.

Get Organised

On your personal computer set up a folder called "my photographs."

When you either take one of yourself or receive one, save it in that folder.

Your Best Angle

There is no correct way of taking a photograph. A good photograph results from paying careful attention to getting the basics right.

Always make sure the photo is in focus and not blurred. Taking a photo of you is a lot easier than strutting yourself on the catwalk. If you were to take 50 photos there bound to be a few that are appealing.

Practice in the mirror beforehand. Try certain facial expressions that you think make you look good and adapt them to your photo.

The human eye travels naturally to the point two thirds of the way up on a picture, therefore proportion of the image must be right.

Make the focus point of the photo the eyes. A person's eyes always tell a story. They convey feelings, emotions and state of mind. Focusing on them will make the photo better project you.

When the picture is taken make sure the person taking the photo angles the camera is slightly upwards. A double chin on a photo is not flattering.

The most flattering angle for most people is when the camera slightly above your head while tilting your face to the side.

Relax and have fun and enjoy yourself.

The Right Location

There should be a plain background that doesn't take away the attention from the person. If you have a dark top on then don't have a dark background and vice versa.

Be sure the only things you want to the viewer see appear in the picture. A busy background will detract from you and your message will be lost if there are too many objects cluttering up the background. Women don't want to see your messy bedroom or bathroom!

You will have more impact if placed against a light/neutral background.

A good example of a good background to use is one of soft solid color like a neutral colored wall in your house. Professional photographers often use indirect light rather than light shining directly on their subject.

Blurring in the background will detract from the profile photo and make the person stand out.

Lighting

It is much better to capture a profile photo in natural light. You will capture the full color range and warmth of the skin.

The profile shot is best taken during the day outside with the sunlight from the side.

Don't take photos with the sun behind you, as you will end like a silhouette.

Don't let the sun be right in front of you as it will be too bright and color will be distorted.

Editing

When uploading your photos there are many free software tools available on-line to edit your pictures. For example Picasa is free and allows such options as taking out red eye or brightening or darkening your photos.

Your Photo for Internet Dating

If you are interested in Internet dating, it is even more important having a selection of good photos in different settings. These photos need to be stand out from "The Pack". Here are a few examples below of popular on-line dating profile shots that are a turn off to women!

The Mirror Shot

A photograph taken by the person in the mirror, especially the bathroom or bedroom mirror. The flash goes off in the mirror and blurs the overall photos making you look distorted and looking like a poser.

Plus these photographs would suggest that you have no friends or that you were in a rush to get your profile on-line! Organise someone to take a shot of you. Offer to take shots of them in return.

The Shirt Off Shot

It is good to emphasis on the parts you like about yourself, like your arms, however keep that shirt on! You may have the best six-pack and abs in the world but women are not going to be dating your body on its own!

If the chemistry is right, you will have plenty of opportunity to reveal all your hard work in the gym. Women would like to see your face first. Instead wear your most flattering shirt or t-shirt that shows off your shape to its best advantage!

The 20 Kilos, 10 Years Younger Shot

Put a recent photograph forward which resembles you. There is nothing more embarrassing than turning up to a date and the woman you are supposed to be meeting is looking around the room trying to find you!

The look of shock when the person she is meeting does not resemble the guy she saw in his photograph could result in an instant run for the hills! You have misrepresented yourself in your photograph, not only that, she will start to wonder what else you may be lying about?

The Long Shot

Taking a photograph from kilometers away when you are a mere dot on the horizon and no one can make out your face, won't attract women either! What are you hiding?

The Black and White Shot

Although some of the best photos have shades of white, grey and black, a woman wants to see what color hair/skin you have. The contrast between colors in a shot is what makes you shine in a photo.

The Animal Shot

A profile photo should only include you. Women want to date you, not your dog or your pet budgie! It is fine to mention them in your profile however; women are only interested in seeing you at this stage. Are they your only friends? Me and the dog, the dog and I!

The Hunter Shot

This image is particularly popular shot within male profiles. A photograph of you on fishing or hunting trip perceived as the "catching a prize trophy shot." It also gives women the impression that you are going to be out with the boys catching fish all weekend!

Guy's, women can catch their own fish.

The Toy's Shot

Women would like to see more photographs of yourself rather than what you have purchased with your cash, whether it be cars, bikes or boats.

Most women today have their own houses, cars, toys and are not fussed seeing you showing off your possessions before they have even met you! What you drive is not important at the point of profile and if it is, do you really want to attract a gold digger? Women want to see photos of you. Again women don't want to date your car!

The Ex Shot

Everyone has had a partner or two! It's a real turn off to see one of these old flames in your profile picture. Even more so, no wedding photos where you have cut out your ex and half her dress!

The Group Shot

Women like to see you in photos on your own. Imagine you have a group photo, it's like playing guess who! Even more so not with your arms around another woman and certainly not kissing. Guys no action shots!

The 'Top Gun' Shot

They may be $500 designer sunglasses you are wearing! If they are covering half of your face women won't get a good idea of what you look like! Plus, a man's eyes and face are of particular interest to a woman when she is deciding if she is attracted to them. This rule applies to baseball caps too!

"The eyes are the windows of the soul". If you are hiding your face especially your eyes, this can cause suspicion with women about your intentions of being on an Internet dating website, like you have something to hide, a girlfriend or a wife!

One shot with sun-glasses is fine as long as there is there are other pictures of you on offer that clearly show your eyes and face.

So guys go and get snapping!

Writing Your On-Line Profile

Don't expect to get your on-line profile perfect the first time. Just to tweak the profile as you go along. It is great to get advice from someone else whose judgment you trust.

Ask them what the profile says to them and whether it describes you or not.

Listen to advice. You don't have to act on it and change anything, just note it for the future in case you decide to alter the profile.

Make notes about your on-line profile what you would like to say before you start fill out the information on the website.

Write From The Heart

It is best to write what comes from the heart. You could sit all day and look at the profiles of other people on-line , you are different - you are not everyone else.

They may look great to you however you have no idea of the responses being received. Therefore copying isn't necessarily a good idea. Women want to have a slight insight to you!

Just Do It

Don't let writing the perfect profile delay you from getting yourself on-line!

Once you are happy with a first draft, get it on-line and see what results you get. You can always amend it later.

On-Line Dating/Choosing The Right Dating Site

There are many different varieties of Internet dating websites with people who are looking for different outcomes. There is everything from casual dating to long-term relationships. If you are just looking for sex initially, there are plenty of websites to go to. Make sure you go for the right one that will suit you. Don't be turned off by having to pay for websites. The people you could be potentially meeting will have also paid!

Your User Name

A username says a lot about a person. For instance, PersonalTrainer2U would suggest that you are a personal trainer or enjoy working out in the gym. Please make sure you use a positive username, not a lame one like Chick Magnet or The Stud!!! Women will skip you for sure and move on to the next profile.

It is important not to use personal information regarding your name, date of birth, address, and personal codes/passwords because of identity fraud.

Choose a name that is reflective of you, perhaps a nickname you once had. If you are into surfing then perhaps include it in your user name, for example Surfnfun.

Write down some user names that you like.

Photograph

Now that you have updated photos, pick out three to five photos. Use the best up close shot of yourself to be your main profile photo. The one that most represents you, makes you feel good when you look at it and the one that you feel will attract the woman you are looking for.

If you are not sure, ask a friend.

Headline

With most dating websites you have to present a catchy headline to attract the reader to click on your profile. Think carefully about this. Do you have a favourite motto that is positive, up beat and sums up your outlook on life? Or perhaps a quote that has inspired you?

It could also capture your personality and sense of humour. It could be a question that intrigues the reader to click and read your profile. The headline, profile name and photo work hand in hand.

Make some notes on headlines that you like.

Keep Your Profile Simple

On-line dating allows you to write down exactly what you want. However, don't get too carried away and write 10 pages of what you are looking for. Not only will your profile be specific in what is and isn't acceptable, you will portray yourself as stiff and shallow!

You will be asked questions ranging from your appearance, to your social likes, dislikes, for example do you smoke? Drink alcohol?

Be specific. The trick here is to paint a big picture about you. Injecting your personality into your profile is a great way of introducing yourself.

Are you a social person? Information about you, your interests these may include music, reading, movies, and sports.

Set yourself apart and mention which movies you like and why you like them. When you are writing about your hobbies and interests elaborate on the story of how you started the particular hobby or interest.

Women want a slight insight of you before potentially meeting you.

 Write down your interests here.

Extra Tips and Tricks for your online profile:-

Here are some of the questions you need to think about.

What do you like doing in your life?

What does your ideal weekend involve?

What are your five most positive traits? If you are unsure ask a friend or family member how they would describe you and why.

What job do you do? It is important to be clear about your hours, if you are on shift work etc.

Honesty

Honesty can eliminate potential people there and then and stop wasting time.

If you have children, then say so. Children are an extremely important part of people's lives and they will affect the next person that comes into your life. If you do not have children and do not wish to date people with children then say so.

Be clear of whom you are and where you want to go.

Be true with your statistics such as weight, height, age, occupation and marital status. You could potentially be setting the foundations of new relationship. This will eliminate time wasters and people who are not looking for what you are.

If you are looking for a long-term relationship say so. There is no point in putting down friendship if you want to remarry.

Keep your profile up beat and positive. Having negative language and comments in your profile will only attract negativity - you don't need in your life!

Put the shoe on the other foot. Write the profile to attract the person you want to meet. Think about what they would find attractive and aim every word at them.

Don't use words in capitals. This implies shouting, I NEED TO MEET SOMEONE WHO IS GORGEOUS!!!!!!!!!!!!

Don't write a list of what you want and a list of time lines, for example I want to meet somebody who wants a baby in the next 2 years!

Avoid The Bland

"I like walking on the beach, dining out and movies."
Everyone does! What does this really tell women about you? Be descriptive about things that are important to you. Instead of "I love my family" say, "I have a great family and we have fun socialising together with games of tennis etc." It sounds much more interesting to the reader.

Understand the impact of your choices.

If you know you only like dating women with blonde hair then mention it in your profile. There is no point wasting your time or any brunette's time.

If you only would like to meet women who have a corporate career then use lingo that is going to attract that particular woman. If you want a casual dating partner or friend rather than a life partner, avoid talking about relationships and the long-term.

A profile that portrays the real you will attract the right person and stop any time wasting on both parties.

What To Remember ...

When you first go into Internet dating you have to realise the women you are chatting too are not exclusive to you just as you are not exclusive to them. In the beginning, most people are going on a few dates with different people every week.

Going into Internet dating looking for your soul mate is putting too much pressure on yourself. Look at is as a way of getting out and meeting new people that you wouldn't have normally come across in your everyday life.

Maybe the person you go on a date with may not spark up chemistry however they may become a great friend. You never know you could always meet someone special through their social circles.

A successful on-line dating profile is only the first step on the journey to finding the friends or the woman of your dreams. Remember what on-line dating really is. It is an opportunity to broaden your contacts and meet some new people of the opposite sex. Realistic expectations and goals will keep your profile interesting and prepare you for the experiences ahead.

Are you ready to start dating again? Are you really over your ex? If you are not sure, here is how you can learn to move forward.

Chapter Nine

Back on the Dating Scene

'Online dating isn't a stigma anymore'
Brenda Ross

What Are You Looking For In A New Partner?

When you are ready to go dating again, think about what you want to gain from dating and the time frames in which you expect to achieve them. Dating can be a time consuming exercise, albeit fun and rewarding on the way, so a big question to ask yourself is, "Do you have the time in your life to go dating?" and if you do have a connection with a woman, do you have the time for a relationship?

Today many women are of the understanding that if you are dating again you have time to pursue a relationship should the chemistry be there. If this is not what you are after, be up front in your profile or when meeting a date for the first time. Make it clear your intentions that you only have time for dating and not a full-blown relationship.

Should you not be ready for anything more than simply friendship with a woman, there are plenty of women out there who would like to go on a date as a friend. They too might have just come out of a long-term relationship and looking to broaden their circle of new friends. The key again is to be honest with yourself and your potential dates.

 What you want from a new partner?

This might seem clinical however, it is important to be clear about what you want from a new relationship. It is not good enough to just go for the opposite of your previous partner or deciding you like young blondes at the moment.

You gain values from many different sources, from your parents/friends, education and religion. Here are some questions that will help you with your decision. Write down your answers in your journal.

Think about your values and evaluate them against those of the person that you are looking to share your life with.

Here are some questions for you to ponder:-

What would you like your future partner to be like?

Do you have room and time in your life for a new partner?

If so what are your long-term goals, 1 year, 3 years and 5 years?

Would you like your partner to be a part of your future goals?

Do you have to travel with work a lot? If yes – where to and what impact could it bring on a new relationship? Would you be allowed to take a partner?

Would you mind if your partner had to travel for work?

Do you want to travel? Where would you like to travel to and when?

Would this include your partner?

How would you like your new partner to interact with your family?

How would you like to interact with your new partner's family?

Does your family have events that you to attend? Would you mind if her family has many get-togethers?

If you have children, do you want more? or if not now, in the future?

Do you want a partner who already has children?

Do you have many friends?

Do you plan weekends away or regular hook ups with your friends or children?

Is it important for your partner to have any friends?

What are your feelings around love and sex?

What would you like your partner's views around love and sex to be?

Dating Again

When you know that you are ready to start dating again, there is a whole new landscape out there to navigate. Most of the basics are the same, boy meets girl, boy likes girl, boy asks girl out on a date or vice versa. However, today there is also a computer involved to help you connect up in the first place.

Communicating with your new potential date

When you have successfully connected with somebody either on-line or through friends, communicating with women today has become more complex. You have the option of using the phone, email, instant messaging, texting and video conferencing.

Remember, just because you are talking to somebody on-line, texting or emailing them, still does not guarantee that you are going to go on a date with them.

A typical way of communicating with your new potential date would be texting if you have her mobile number or emailing if you have her email address to arrange a time to talk. Then you can call her and have a chat. If you feel there is a connection, ask her to meet up. Or if you are getting along well and she feels comfortable enough, she might as you!

As you are talking, you can find out the types of places that she would like to meet up.

Like mentioned earlier, the days of picking up somebody up from their house on the first date are long gone. Today it is better to arrange to meet at the destination.

It is usual to meet up for a quick coffee or a drink first to see how you get on in person. If you have an evening date and you think you are getting along then perhaps suggest having dinner or even the movies in case the nerves have got the better of you. At least then after the film you have something to talk about.

The day before, confirm that your date is still able to make the date. If a change is unavoidable, be respectful and do not be negative about it. Life can be busy at times!

If for some reason you cannot make the date, make sure you personally call her (don't just send a text), well in advance to cancel. Suggest another couple of days that you are free to meet so the date can be rescheduled.

Check the location on a map and make sure you know how to get there and be on time.

You could look this up on-line Where Is also offer to send the info to your date via email.

Make sure you know how to get there yourself and plan your route. Check if there will be heavy traffic or if there is a special event on in the area (like a football game) at the same time.

Always Dress Smartly

You want to make a good impression. This person could be a part of your future life. Everyone needs to look their best.

Dress Within Your Character

Always dress within your character. The basic idea is to start smart then gradually incorporate a more individual style. You might think your favourite Hawaiian shirt expresses your personality however it may be best to leave this one for the fancy dress beach parties!

Make Sure Your Clothes Are Free Of Creases

Running a hot iron over your clothes only takes a couple of minutes and will make such a difference to your overall appearance. There is nothing worse than looking like you have just rolled out of bed. Leave the house with ironed clothes showing that you have made an effort!

Clean Shoes

Make sure that your shoes are clean and polished. If you are going on a date where you are going to wear your trainers, you can get rid of any nasty smells by putting baking powder into the soles the day before.

If you are going on a date where you'll be wearing thongs or pluggers make sure that your feet are presentable. There is nothing worse than werewolf feet! Pedicure time!

Dress Fashionably

Fashion is ever changing and what looks great on one person may not on another. Take into consideration today's fashion is important. Mixing it with your own sense of style will keep you up to date with the times and will work wonders for your look and confidence.

Check Before You Leave The House

Look at yourself in the mirror and decide what you like and do not like. Emphasize your body parts that you like and disguise the parts you don't like.

Dressing For The Location Of The Date

Depending on where you are going will help you decide what to wear. If it is the movies, casual wear will be fine. Dinner will incorporate a bit more effort, perhaps smart jeans or trousers and a nice shirt. The days of the white tuxedo and black tie have long gone!

Be Confident

Walking into a room with your head held high, feeling great, knowing that your hair, skin, teeth, clothing, shoes and hands are clean will give you a spring in your step that commands attention.

Confidence is the best way to make people notice you. Be confident and proud of your body. You look better in clothing when you feel confident. Stand tall with your shoulders back, have good posture, carry yourself well and smile. Women love confidence!

On The Day Of The Date

On the day of the date, watch or listen to the news, even look up general interesting stories on the Internet. At least then you have some prepared topics of conversation. It will help to make the woman feel comfortable if you talk about third party external topics and events. Subjects that are not related to either of you make good talking points. Save asking more personal questions for later if you are both getting on.

Always steer clear of religious or political topics until you get to know them better. Many people feel very passionate about these subjects, which can lead to heated conversations, not a great start on a first date!

Other topics to steer clear of are your ex-girlfriend, ex-wives, ex-mistress, in fact - all ex's. If you hear yourself starting to say something like – "oh! my ex used to do/say/wear that . . . . " and the other person just listens, this does not mean that you have permission to continue talking about your ex.
It just means that this woman is too kind to scream at the top of her voice "FOR GODS SAKE DON'T TALK TO ME ABOUT YOUR PREVIOUS PARTNERS".

Instead she is likely to finish the date as soon as possible, call her girlfriend's straight afterwards and say "Yep – another one bites the dust – he talked about his ex – so boring!".

From the research we compiled for this book, talking about your ex is the number one turn off for a woman.

Security

For no other reason than common sense, always tell a friend or family member where you are going and who you are going to meet.

If you are planning a date straight after work, plan ahead and take a clean shirt with you and change beforehand. Make sure you freshen up. Doing this will also make you feel better, lift your energy levels and make you feel more confident about the encounter!

Don't overdo it on the first date with flowers or chocolates or any gifts. There will be plenty of time for that if you have chemistry and continue to see each other. These days, over the top gestures are likely to put a woman off and you will come across like you are trying too hard.

In the minutes before a date, spend some time thinking about what you want to know about the person.

Think of the date as a casual try out or interview to see if both of you are compatible. Ask questions that will help you determine if you would like to go on a second date or not.

If you want to reduce your nervousness, exercise before the date. Do 30 minutes of cardiovascular exercise and you will be more relaxed, or course shower afterwards. And in addition to being relaxed, you will also receive a nice endorphin high. This will put yourself in a positive mood, bringing out the confident guy within you.

If you have your dates on an evening time, it is good to get in the habit of exercising late afternoon. That way, you will become used to having that particular endorphin high right around the time you are going to be meeting up with your date and reduce nervous energy.

Write down a list of activities that you can do before a date to help you feel more relaxed and confident.

Overcoming Nerves

'We were having one of those great first dates you can only have when it's not an actual date"

Sarah Jessica Parker

The thought of going on a first date with someone new can be overwhelming. It is important to keep everything in perspective and you must always be prepared and alert.

You may have chatted to someone on the phone and had a few text messages. However many people are different when you meet them in person. A telephone can mask a lot including the confidence of the woman you are meeting. Remember, she may well be feeling the same as you.

This can present itself in different ways. For instance- your heart may beat a little faster, your blood pressure could rise, you could start to sweat a little and your stomach could get butterflies. That's fine you are after all human!

You could be afraid that you may stumble over your words or even say the wrong thing, can make your confidence spiral downwards. A drink may help calm the nerves, do not have more than one or two though you don't want to be slurring your words!

Questions

If you loosely work out in advance what possible situations may come up in any potential scenarios, you will be prepared for whatever may arise.

To help you with this, prepare a few open-ended questions. These include questions starting with Who, What, How, When, Where and Why.

When you start a conversation with any of these, the woman is far more likely to give you a detailed answer which can lead on to the next question. Instead of closed questions that only require a yes or no answer as they can shut the flow of conversation down.

Breathing

An excellent yoga technique to help stay calm is to breathe in for four seconds and out for four seconds. Feel your diaphragm (the bit under your ribs – near your belly button) inhale and gently, exhale.

Think of something that calms you down, the beach, the ocean, being outside. Take a deep breath before arrive at the place you are meeting. It will help relax you.

Be positive

You are our thoughts, so think positive thoughts! Even if there is no chemistry between you and your potential date, be nice and friendly as you never know, you could end up becoming good friends. And through her you could be introduced to your next long-term girlfriend!

It can be a small world and just because you do not know the person does not mean that you should be rude. You never know where your paths might cross in the future.

Be Confident

Be yourself and be interesting. With your new hobbies and social activities, you should have plenty to talk about.

Most of all enjoy you and have fun.

During your first date

"It's much easier to become interested in others than it is to convince them to be interested in you."
Dale Carnegie

By taking the time to consider all the parts of a date before you go, will help you prepare, thus making you feel more relaxed and give you the head space to enjoy your time together.

First off is . . .

First Impressions

Practice your handshake. You should reach out grasp the other persons hand firmly without crushing their fingers and then release. The amount of men who don't realise that when they shake a woman's hand it is normally small and dainty!

Shake hands immediately upon being introduced to someone new, and say the other person's name, along with, "Hi, it's nice to meet you" looking the person straight in the eyes.

Eye Contact

When you are talking keep looking every now and again at that persons eyes, especially when they are talking. And don't lean in too close while you are still getting to know each other. It makes us feel uncomfortable and invades our personal space!

Be A Gentleman

Being a gentleman is sure to impress any woman you're interested in.

Easy things to do are, either pull out your date's chair or at least stand up if you are sitting down when she comes into the room.

Treat women chivalrously, don't be condescending!

When initiating physical contact other than the initial handshake, take it slow. Don't touch a person until you know them better.

If you ask a woman out on a date, offer to pay for dinner. Your date may offer to go Dutch or halves, this is fine. This is often a sign of a no strings attached evening and that she prefers to leave in an even way.

Alternatively if she accepts your offer, then you can lead into testing the water to see if she would like to see you again by saying she can get can get the bill next time.

Take it easy on the alcohol. Your judgment about the other person will be skewed the more you drink. Many a date has started off with two people not that sure about each other, apply vodka and voila in it could end up with you both in bed! Which is fine, just means it can be awkward when really, if you were sober you would not have been romantically involved with that person.

Never act as though all you are interested in sex or try to initiate sex unless the other person has given you crystal clear signals to do so. If you are not sure what those signals are, then you are not getting them!

One dating tip is - guys keep that ego down!! Don't let it become a night of focusing on you!

Don't be too serious or too over the top. Being too serious won't make it the date fun. Just be yourself and don't try to impress too much. Both of you will end up learning a lot about each other and keeping the communication alive.

Another tip is, even if Megan Fox walks into the joint or serves you at the bar, do not flirt with her, give here the eye or keep starring over at her! It might seem too obvious to mention, making comments about other women in the room but it has happened. A particularly good statement to avoid is, 'I wouldn't mind giving her one'. NO !

The most important dating tip is to just be you! "People buy People not the product"

Great Conversations And Active Listening

The art of conversation takes practice and is not as hard as you might think. It will take some knowledge, time and patience.

Most importantly, LISTEN. This is key to any conversation. Pay attention to what is being said.

A conversation will not go anywhere if you are too busy thinking of something else, this includes what you plan to say next. If you listen well the other person's statements will suggest questions in your mind for you to ask.

Allow the other person to do most of the talking. They will often not realise that it was themselves who did most of the talking. People like to talk about themselves and you will get the credit for being a good conversationalist - which of course, you are.

Find out what the other person is interested in. You can even do some research in advance on the phone or via email. Then research the interest and when the opportunity arises then you are armed to talk about it.

If you are too busy thinking about yourself, what you look like, or what the other person might be thinking, you will never be able to relax. Introduce yourself, shake hands, then forget yourself and focus on them instead.

Complimenting them is a great place to start. Everyone likes sincere compliments, and that can be a great icebreaker.

Ask questions. What do they like to do in their spare time? What experiences have they had in their lives? What is happening to them now? What did they do today or last weekend? Where have they been and or going on holidays?

Identify things about them that you might be interested in hearing about and politely ask questions. Remember, there was a reason why you wanted to talk to them, so obviously there was something about them that you found interesting!

Try to space out your questions or they could feel like you're interrogating them and shut down a conversation.

Active Listening

Learning active listening skills is about letting the other person know that you are listening. Make eye contact. Nod and make affirming comments like "Yes", "that's interesting", "I agree" to give them clues you are paying attention.

Ask clarifying questions. If the topic is one they are clearly passionate about, ask them to clarify what they think or feel about it. If they are talking about an occupation or a pastime you don't understand, take the opportunity to learn from them. Don't be a 'know it all' when you are not 100% sure about the topic they are talking about. Just ask the question "Can you please explain more about that to me?"

Everyone loves having the chance to teach another willing and interested person about their hobby or subject of expertise.

Paraphrase back what you have heard. This is when you use your own words to describe what has just been said to you. This seems like an easy skill to learn however, can take some time to master. Conversation happens in turns with each person taking a turn to listen and a turn to speak or to respond.

It shows respect for the other person when you use your "speaking turn" to show you have been listening and not just to say something new. They then have a chance to correct your understanding, affirm it, or enhance it. Consider your response before disagreeing. If the point was not important, ignore it rather than risk appearing argumentative. If you consider it important, then politely point out your difference of opinion. Do not disagree merely to set yourself apart.

Points To Remember About Conversations.

1. It is the differences in people and their conversation that make them interesting.

2. Agreeing with everything can kill a conversation just as easily as disagreeing with everything.

3. A person is interesting when they are different from you. A person is obnoxious when they cannot agree with anything you say or if they use the point to make themselves appear superior.

4. Try to omit the word "but" from your conversation when disagreeing as this word often gets people on the wrong side. Instead try substituting the word "and" as it has less of an antagonistic effect.

5. Consider playing devil's advocate that requires care. If your date makes a point you can keep the conversation going by bringing up the opposite point of view (introduce it with something like "I agree, and..."). If you over use this technique you could end up appearing disagreeable or even hostile.

6. Do not panic over lulls. This is a point where you could easily inject your thoughts into the discussion. If the topic has run out, use the pause to think for a moment and identify another conversation topic or question to ask them. Be relaxed!

7. Did something they said remind you of something else you have heard, something that happened to you, or bring up a question or topic in your mind? Mention it and you'll transition smoothly into further conversation.

8. Know when the conversation is over. Even the best conversations will eventually run out of steam or be interrupted. Smile if you're leaving and let them know if you'd like to see them again. Ending on a positive note will leave a good impression and likely bring your date back for more!

Don't be worried about the conversation and where it will go. People have natural conversation reflexes. Thinking too much will make an awkward conversation that is difficult to keep going.

Try to lead into personal stories and anecdotes. These give limitless conversation and are revealing about the character of a person.

It's okay to talk about yourself as long as the person listening is interested and getting new information about you or the topic. People don't like to go over topics they already know or have thought about so try to give a new perspective or way of thinking if you're the one speaking.

Always think before you speak, just for a second! Do not take a long time to answer and listen well to keep on the right track with the conversation.

Avoid giving an opinion that may disrespect someone else. Choose your words carefully. Do not create pointless silences by keeping your conversation partner waiting for five minutes before you answer a simple question!

Remember that sometimes if a conversation isn't going well, it might not be your fault. Sometimes the other person is distracted/lost in thought, isn't willing to contribute or is having a bad day. If they don't speak or listen, then they're the ones who are not using good conversation skills, not you.

Choose carefully when asking questions. You don't want to venture into personal issues. Even if the other person is willing to talk about it, you may learn new things that you don't want to know. You don't want the other person to think afterwards that you lead them into revealing personal information that they were not comfortable sharing!

Make Your Date Feel Comfortable - Build Rapport

Have you ever felt an instant connection with a woman?

Sparks are flying and you feel like you've known her forever? Well this connection is "rapport."

So what is rapport and how can you use it to build attraction with a woman?

In a dating sense, rapport is defined as two people who are in sync with one another and feel heightened levels of attraction. When rapport occurs, a man or woman feels a high level of trust with the other person and it can lead to an intimate experience.

When you establish rapport with a woman it then makes both people fee relaxe and if everything is going well it can be easier to ask her out on another date.

Ways To Build Rapport When You Meet A Woman:

1. Discussing common interests and hobbies.

2. Flirting and establishing physical contact.

3. Teasing her in a fun manner.

4. Mirroring her actions and sending open body language signals.

5. Having an attractive personality and bringing up interesting topics.

If you can quickly build rapport with a woman, you'll be on the road towards building attraction and making her interested in you.

Another way to build rapport with another person is having a better understanding of body language.

What Is Body Language?

Body language, no this is not reading bodies and running your eyes up and down ours! Is a non-verbal communication that consists of a combination of body position, eye movements and hand gestures.

A human sends and interpret signals unconsciously. According to John Borg, who wrote "Body Language, 7 easy Lessons to Master the Silent Language" human communication is made up of 93% body language, while only 7% of how we communicate is made up of words.

A simple example of this is when somebody is telling you a story and they fail to make eye contact with you while doing so. You get an uneasy feeling that they are hiding something. So establishing eye contact creates trust between two people.

One of the most basic and powerful body language signals is when a person crosses his or her arms across the chest. This can indicate that a person is putting up an unconscious barrier between themselves and others. It can also simply indicate the person's arms are cold which rubbing the arms or huddling would clarify.

When the overall situation is friendly it can mean that a person is thinking deeply about what is being discussed. However, in a serious or confrontational situation, it can mean that a person is expressing opposition. This is especially so if the person is leaning away from the person who is talking. If you combine this gesture with a blank expression your conversation could potentially be hostile.

Consistent eye contact can mean that a person is thinking positively of what the speaker is saying. It can also mean the other person doesn't trust the speaker enough to "take his eyes off" the speaker.

Lack of eye contact can indicate negativity. On the other hand individuals with anxiety disorders are often unable to make eye contact without discomfort. Eye contact is often a secondary and misleading gesture as from an early age people are taught to make eye contact when speaking.

If a person is looking at you and making the arms-across-chest signal, the eye contact could be indicative that something is bothering the person and they want to talk about it. Or if while making direct eye contact a person is fiddling with something, even while directly looking at you, it could indicate the attention is elsewhere.

There are three standard areas that a person will look which represent different states of being. If the person looks from one eye to the other then to the forehead, it is a sign that they are taking an authoritative position. If they move from one eye to the other then to the nose that signals that they are engaging in what they consider to be a "level conversation" with neither party holding superiority. The last case is from one eye to the other and then down to the lips. This is a strong hint of romantic feelings.

Boredom can be indicated by the head tilting to one side or by the eyes looking straight at the speaker and becoming slightly unfocused. On the other hand a head tilt may also simply mean a sore neck.

Here are some simple examples not to be taken too literally more in general: -

- Hands on knees: indicates readiness.
- Hands on hips: indicates impatience.
- Lock your hands behind your back: indicates self-control.
- Locked hands behind head: states confidence.
- Sitting with a leg over the arm of the chair: suggests indifference.
- Legs and feet pointed in a particular direction: the direction where more interest is felt
- Crossed arms: indicates submissiveness.

You can read up more on body language as there are plenty of great books on the topic. This was just a taste to help you understand more about people in general and also to assist you understand the non-verbal signals that your date is sending you.

So when you're talking to a woman, try to focus on building rapport and reading a little bit of her body language. If you can do this successfully, you'll master conversations and will be able to quickly establish instant connections.

Flirting

First of all let's look at what is flirting? Flirting is a common form of social interaction whereby one person obliquely indicates a romantic and/or sexual interest towards another. It can consist of conversation, body language or brief physical contact. It may be one-sided or reciprocated (encouraged).

A Few tips on flirting to run alongside body language

1. Maintain Eye Contact

Keeping eye contact whilst talking shows you are interested in her - not staring and vice versa. If you have a habit of looking around a room you will put her off so help yourself and position your line of sight towards a wall when you sit down.

2. A Cheeky Smile

One of the most effective flirting tips for men is to add in a cheeky smile when you are talking to a woman. The cheeky smile is not an 'over the top' type of smile. It's confident, relaxed and a little bit mischievous. Try it now in front of the mirror, can you carry it off?

3. Compliments

Women like to be complimented on their appearance, clothes, hair, eyes etc. Whatever you like about them tell them, make sure it is genuine and you will win brownie points.

4. Be Playful

Seeing the light side of life and making jokes to make a woman laugh is a great way to show you are interested in her and that you like to be funny.

5. Lightly Touch

Gently brush her arm or leg. It's sexy and frisky without being overbearing. This is great to do when you are talking, perhaps sharing a story. You could say something like "Let me tell you about the time... " and while saying this you could touch her on the arm.

There is an illusion out there with men that flirting = sex. Many women are natural flirts and love to flirt with men and women. It is part of our nature! Flirting usually makes both people feel good, however, it is not a 100% iron clad guarantee that they will want to jump into bed with you!

Flirting is fun, enjoy it! When you get it right you can have a great time and put smiles on many faces!

At The End Of The First Date

"The best way to find your perfect match is to meet love halfway."

Anonymous

As your first date is coming to a close there is the chance you could be rejected, or perhaps you're the one who is going to say, "No thanks" to another date . . .

Here are some questions to keep in mind towards the end of the date: -

Do you want to see this person again?

Does it feel like she wants to see you again?

You might not know at this stage and would like to keep your options open.

Be Honest!

Be straight with how you feel about the other person. Thank your date for a wonderful time and leave it at that. If she isn't right for you then it's better to deal with it now rather than later and string her along.

As it happens, most people appreciate honesty. Don't just dump your feelings on them. Keep it short and sweet.

Some people find it hard to say "no" in person and end up stringing people along as they don't want to hurt the other person's feelings. In this case you will end up hurting them more by pretending you like them when you don't. Be responsible and kind and let the other person know.

You never know where your paths may cross again and just because you haven't made a romantic connection, there is always potential to be friends. She may have plenty of single friends that she could put you in touch with. Therefore even more of a reason to be polite, honest and considerate of her feelings!

If you have enjoyed your date, tell her. There is no need to be shy about the situation. If you liked their company, let them know that you would like to spend more time with them.

Say, "I had a great time and I'd like to do it again soon." Most women usually expect to hear from a man the next day or two. Let's face it when you are keen on someone, nothing can stop you from picking up the phone.

Based on information we gathered, it seems men tend to make contact within 48 hours if they are interested in seeing their date again. Women tend to like contact the day after to say thank you or to indicate you'd like to go on another date. A text is fine saying you had a great time.

Everyone knows the feeling when you have a great connection with somebody you can't wait to speak to them again. Watch out for leaving it for 5 or more days as it will indicate you are not bothered!

Don't be clingy or mention anything remotely connected to commitment or future plans. You are still getting to know each other, so take it one step at a time.

Let's Just Be "Friends"

You met firstly and foremost for romance with the possibility of starting a relationship. Some people may not be interested in being friends because they are after something deeper than a platonic relationship.

On the flip side of the coin, if you have got on well and there is clearly no physical attraction, then the suggestion of friends could be on the cards. You can never have too many friends!

Do Ask For Another Date . . . If You Want To!

If you really like the person, you feel you have got on well, you have read all the signals correctly and you feel she is feeling the same way too, ask for a second date.

If You Are Slightly Unsure

It is better to keep it light hearted and relaxed. If you feel your date is less interested than yourself, then it is easier to keep your options open. That way your date will have time to consider. Perhaps suggest meeting up again sometime with no specific date in mind.

Leaving The Date On A High Note

By leaving on a high point rather than a low one you will give your date a better impression of you and your date will look forward to seeing you again – if that is would both like to!

Again, just to re-emphasise this is not about giving your date a false impression of wanting to meet up with them again if you don't! If you are not interested in pursuing a second date it is still good to end on a positive note!

Examples Of Ways To End The Date On A Positive Now Are:-

1. I had a lovely time with you – thank you!

2. That was a fantastic meal

3. That was a great movie

4. Thank you for some great conversation.

5. Pay your date a compliment about something that they were wearing, perhaps, "You looked great this evening."

These statements are also a great way of leading into asking her out on another date if you really would like to see her again. For example "that was a great movie, we should do this again soon?" or "what would you like to see next time?".

Body Language / Flirting

As discussed earlier in the book, understanding body language and a bit of flirting can help you assess how the other person is feeling towards the end of the date.

If she's got her arms crossed or her hands in her bag trying to find her keys or she tries to bolt out the door before you can make a move, she is not interested!

If in doubt, stay away from kissing until you receive stronger signals. It is acceptable for someone who has felt the date has not gone so well to offer a handshake as a goodwill gesture.

Even a hug or a peck on the cheek is fine.

Strong sexual advances too early are a big turnoff and often can make the person feel uncomfortable.

Comfort Zone

Even if you think the date went well and there is the potential of romance. Do not make a move on her if it is not within your comfort zone.

Do Not Assume Sex

Dating is a gradual process. Your date will most probably want to keep their mystery or keep you interested by prolonging the sexual tension between you both.

If there is sexual chemistry between you both then it is great to wait a while and let the attraction simmer.

See Your Date Is Safely On Their Way Home.

Escort your date safely to a cab or to her car. By doing this you are showing courtesy and manners and that you are considerate of her welfare.

Follow Up

If you feel you have got on well with your date a great gesture is to send a text or an email thanking them for a lovely evening. If they respond, you will know that is was reciprocal!

Multi-Dating

As mentioned before, you may have a few dates before you meet someone you like or who is compatible. You have to appreciate that most people who Internet date are chatting to other people, if not meeting up with them too.

If that sounds like something you would like to do great, that's fine, it's a personal preference.

When multi dating you are not only meeting new people who could widen your social circle, you increase the chances of you meeting the woman of your dreams.

So if you get the "let's just be friends" line you can move on easily to the next date.

It is fine to chat about other dates and experiences you have had. However don't mention the new person is in a chain of 10 and you are deciding which one to pick!

Chapter Ten

What next?

"You can't change the past but you can ruin the present by worrying about the future"

Anon

Congratulations on taking the first few brave steps to changing your life and becoming the new improved you. This book and its steps are to be used as a guide only. Everyone has their own individual strengths and weaknesses. In fact, some of the outlined steps you will already be exceptional at! More skills taken on board will determine a better outcome for you.

Keep all your notes with this book so you can keep coming back to them and monitoring your progress. This book and your notes are a tool to gaining your confidence back and setting you back on track to join the dating world.

You may be feeling a little overwhelmed or thinking where do I start? We have put together 7 steps in 7 weeks program that breaks down the whole book into a simple easy to follow process.

7 Steps in 7 Weeks

Steps	Week One	Yes	Week Two	Yes	Week Three	Yes	Week Four	Yes	Week Five	Yes	Week Six	Yes	Week Seven	Yes
Step One Confidence	Write down how you feel & list positives about yourself		Focus on a new picture, ie an outfit or an activity, take new photos & show a friend						Positive language and thoughts – watch your words and listen to your inner voice		Practise the Eye Confidence Trick every day this week		Ask a woman you fancy out on a date	
Step Two Hobbies & Interests	Write down things you enjoy & activities you used to do, pick one and start again		Research the hobby or activity more & plan how to get involved		Take the necessary steps to get involved in the hobby/activity		Just do it – sign up and participate in your new hobby/activity		Practise, Practise, and more Practise – remember it makes Perfect !		Update your online profiles with your new activity choice		Does the new club have a social group? If so get involved. Also join Online groups that are interested in this activity	
Step Three Social & Friends	Make a list of who you would like to spend time with & how often		Make sure you would like to meet up at some point with all these people		Get in touch with them to arrange meetings & times		Get in touch, send them an email or give them a call or write there a note		Make plans to meet up with your friends again in the future		Maintain contact, keep in touch online or on the phone		Plan an activity that you can do together – bike, night out, perhaps with a few more friends	
Step Four Fitness & Nutrition	Look at ways you can incorporate physical activity into every day, take the stairs instead of the lift, or get off the bus stop a couple of stops before your home one. Make a list of bad foods in your diet and work to eliminate as many as you can		Do some light exercise - like walking for 20 mins 3 times per week. Make a list of good foods and work to include them in your weekly diet		Increase your light exercise to 30 mins and do it 4 times this week. Take a note of your trigger food emotions - do you eat more when you are happy and less when you are down? What do you eat? Make a list		Add some variety to your fitness regime - go to the gym or go for a swim? Look at some recipes for some dishes that you would like to cook		Write your fitness contract. Practise cooking one of your new dishes. Spend a couple of hours going through your wardrobe and culling old clothes - be ruthless and donate to charity the ones that are no longer in good condition. Get rid of the old to make space for the new		Get a workout buddy and plan your fitness sessions with them. Plan one day to cook two dishes, make 3 portions and freeze the remainder to help you get organised		Go to the Doctor and have a full body check up. Invite one of your friends over for dinner and cook them one of your new dishes	
Step Five Taking Care of Yourself	Have a think about ways that you could take care of yourself that would improve your image, ask a friend or family member for advice		Treat yourself to some new skin lotion for your face		Now, be honest, any rearranging needed?		Look at a new hairstyle or is it time to add a beard or get rid of one?		Look at your body shape and write a list of new clothes that you are going to buy. Research spa treatments that appeal to you		Go shopping for new clothes and treat yourself to a spa treatment			
Step Six Online World	Research what Social Media Websites you would like to be part of		Take some new photos in different settings and with different clothes – remember the rules 1:1:1		Before you start filling out the online forms write some notes about what you would like to say about yourself & your username		Spend some time thinking about what you want from a new partner and write it down		Get online and put your profile up there on the websites that you have chosen.		Start chatting to people online and have some fun.			
Step Seven Dating Again	Write down what you believe were the contributing factors to your previous relationships breaking down. Accept responsibility for your past. Now acknowledge that it is in the past.		Practise reading other people's body language at work and in social situations – then when you feel ready start working on building rapport.		Work on your listening skills with friends and family – ask open ended questions – who, what, when, where, why and how to gather information and become great at having conversations.		Get flirty - practise flirting with people you meet in coffee shops - make eye contact and while you don't be cheeky. Have fun !		Get together a list of places that you would like to go on a date, check out what is on in your town and put it in your calendar - you will impress your future date by being in the know.		Overcoming Nerves! Be prepared – think about what you are going to say on a date and practise breathing techniques.		Start spending time thinking about what you would like to meet up with in person? Ask them on a date.	

Copy the chart, for your own personal use only, put it on your wall and tick off each step as you complete it. The chart is color-coded red, amber, green, yes that's right just like a traffic light!!

Red means stop, slow down and think, focus on yourself and work through as many of the 7 steps as you can if it takes longer than 7 weeks that is ok too.   Amber engage, get ready to,

and green, go for it – if you feel you are ready get back out there and start dating again.

All of us who have been involved with The Single Man's Manual wish you the very best and hope you enjoy every step of this exciting new journey.

The Single Man's manual website is

www.thesinglemanslifemanual.com

Wishing you all the best for your future.

Clodagh, Sarah and our team of guys.

This book was written by us and our team of male advisors who have all been through the breakdown of a long-term relationship. Their insights and intimate personal knowledge of how they suddenly found themselves single again, provides the backbone of the advice given in this book.

Clodagh Samantha Higgins

Originally from Ireland, Clodagh moved to Australia in 1999 and is a NLP Certified Coach. She has a diploma in Frontline Management and currently owns and runs a Business Services Consultancy in Sydney, specialising in Online Social Media. Prior to that, Clodagh spent 15 years in the corporate sector in Ireland and the UK. When she is not working, Clodagh likes four wheel driving, creating mosaics, yoga and listening to music – loud!

Sarah Louise Rutherford

Born in Newcastle upon Tyne. Sarah moved to Australia in 2007. Sarah has a Higher National Diploma in Business and Finance with Marketing and currently works in the Corporate Arena as a Sales Professional. Prior to that, Sarah spent 3 years in Spain and 10 years in the corporate sector in the UK. When Sarah is not working, she loves to travel and explore new places, painting and kick boxing.

Sarah & Clodagh met in 2008 when their careers took them to the same company. As their friendship grew, they realised they had very similar life experiences and had both spent time on the single dating scene in Sydney.

After many conversations with friends and colleagues, they saw the need for The Single Man's Manual. a book giving straightforward advice to men from women to help them feel great from the inside out. The tool for inventing a fabulous new life with many tips including- how to date again.

They could not have written it without the input from their team of guys who gave them an insight to their relationship break ups and how they coped.

The Single Man's Manual

How do pick yourself up after the breakdown of a long-term relationship?

How do you make the most of starting your life over?

What is the best way to find new friends?

For men struggling to cope with a failed relationship, there is now help.

The Single Man's manual is a simple manual, including a 7 steps in 7 weeks program, full of practical tips and straight forward advice to help change your life from the inside out.

You will be shown how to plan your new future for yourself. A future that will have you feeling positive and excited.

A Single Man's manual covers everything from fitness and nutrition, to re entering the world of relationships, including advice from women on dating in the new on-line world.

Please note that much of this publication is based on personal experience and anecdotal evidence. Although the authors and publisher have made every reasonable attempt to achieve complete accuracy of the content in this Manual, they assume no responsibility for errors or omissions. Also, you should use this information as you see fit, and at your own risk. Your particular situation may not be exactly suited to the examples illustrated here; in fact, it's likely that they won't be the same, and you should adjust your use of the information and recommendations accordingly.

Any trademarks, service marks, product names or named features are assumed to be the property of their respective owners, and are used only for reference. There is no implied endorsement if we use one of these terms.

Finally, use your head. Nothing in this Manual is intended to replace common sense, legal, medical or other professional advice, and is meant to inform and entertain the reader. So have fun with The Single Man's manual, and enjoy your new life!